A Nelson Intensive English

Compact

Elementary

Student's and Practice Book

Debra Powell *with*
Madeline McHugh

Nelson

Contents and Map of the Book

SS = Student's Section PS = Practice Section GR = Grammar Reference TS = Tapescripts

UNIT 1

Make a date!

1 *Saying what you think*

a Look at the people in the pictures. Are they saying hello or goodbye? Do you greet/say goodbye to friends, family, strangers, work colleagues in different ways?

b Look at these expressions. Which are for a) meeting people b) leaving people? Do you know any more expressions like these?

Bye Cheerio! Goodbye Good morning
Good night Hello! Hi! How are you?
How do you do? Pleased to meet you
See you later See you soon

2 *Personal information*

a **This is a form for an agency that finds friends for people. Read the form and describe a) Renato Cesar b) his ideal friend.**

b **Listen to Josette filling in her form at the agency. Write down her personal details.**

c **Now listen to Part 2 and describe Josette. Is she a good friend for Renato? Why?/Why not?**

	Yourself	Ideal friend
Surname	CESAR	
First name	RENATO	
Address	275 DORMER RD LONDON	
Sex	M ☐ F ☐ (please tick)	M ☐ F ☐ (please tick)
Nationality	BRAZILIAN	ANY
Occupation	ENGINEER	NOT IMPORTANT
Marital Status	☐ SINGLE ☐ MARRIED ☐ DIVORCED	
Age	27	25–30
Height	183 CM	NOT IMPORTANT
Interests:	Sport ☐ Music ☐ Travel ☐ Theatre ☐	
Other	PHOTOGRAPHY	ANY
Personality:	Friendly ☐ Shy ☐ Fashionable ☐ Other ☐ Smoker ☐ Non-smoker ☐	FRIENDLY, NON-SMOKER

3 *Language focus*

present simple in questions

a **Look at these examples:**

1 *What's* your surname?
2 *How* old *are* you?
3 *What do* you do?
4 *Are you* interested in travel?
5 *Do you* like classical music?

Make similar questions with these words.

address? married? interested in . . . ? tall . . . ? smoke?

b **Find the questions above which can take the following answers.**
a) Yes, I am./No I'm not. b) Yes, I do./No, I don't.
Write five questions for answer a) and five questions for answer b).

Example a) Are you Spanish? — Yes, I am.
b) Do you live in Paris? — No, I don't

4 *Ideal friends*

a Look at the form in exercise 2. Ask and answer questions in pairs. Complete the form with details of your partner's ideal friend.

Example How tall is she/he?
What does he/she do? } — It doesn't matter.
Is she/he interested in photography? — Yes she is.

b Now work in groups and exchange forms with everyone in your group. Can you find an ideal friend for yourself?

A

B

PERSONAL

1 •**Friendly man,** 28, enjoys eating out. Plays a lot of sport.Looking for a friend (male or female) with similar interests. Must be a non-smoker. Reply to Dan, Box No 42.

2 •**Two girls,** 18 and 19, want to meet two others (male or female) who enjoy walking, squash and conversation. Letters please to Gemini, Box No 41.

3 •**Young, fit and trendy man,** 25, likes pop music and going to discos and the cinema. Wants friends with similar interests. Will answer all letters with photo. Reply to Bill, Box No 45.

C

D

5 *Small ads*

a Read the advertisements and match them with the photographs.

b Now read some extracts from letters answering the advertisements. Which ones do they answer?

1

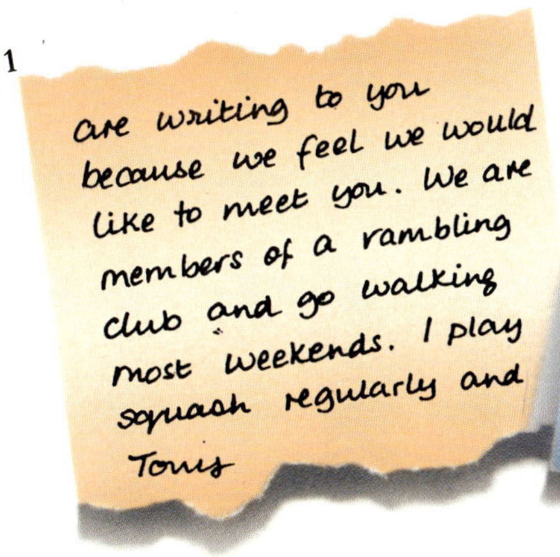

are writing to you because we feel we would like to meet you. We are members of a rambling club and go walking most weekends. I play squash regularly and Tony

2

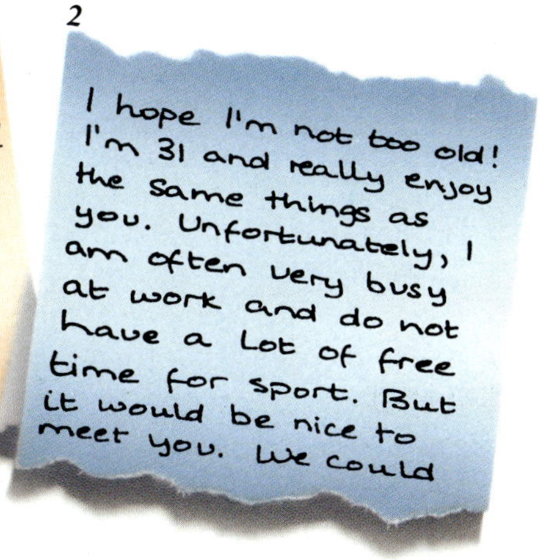

I hope I'm not too old! I'm 31 and really enjoy the same things as you. Unfortunately, I am often very busy at work and do not have a lot of free time for sport. But it would be nice to meet you. We could

c Write an advertisement describing yourself and the kind of people you would like to meet.

6 *Small talk*

a Listen to the five conversations. What is the relationship of the speakers in each conversation? Think of: friends, family, colleagues at work.

b Where does each conversation take place?

office restaurant home street shop

c Look at the expressions in 1b. Tick the ones you hear.

7 *Vocabulary*

Match the headings with the information.

SURNAME	Anna Brown
FIRST NAME	071 – 446 – 318
SIGNATURE	BROWN
NATIONALITY	ANNA
HOME ADDRESS	12 – 8 – 69
TELEPHONE NUMBER	BRITISH
DATE OF BIRTH	21, HOLLY LANE, LONDON.

UNIT 2

Home and family

1 *Saying what you think*

a Match the photographs with some of the words below. Which country do you think each home is in? Which ones are suitable for family life?

house windmill caravan flat houseboat

b In pairs, ask and answer questions about homes.

Example Where do you live?
What kind of home do you live in?
Who do you live with?

2 *A home of my own*

a Listen to three people talking about where they live. Match a photograph from exercise 1 with each speaker.

b Complete sentences which are true for the speakers in dialogues A, B and C.

1 I live	with my family. with friends. by myself.	3 It has got	one room. three bedrooms. three bathrooms.
2 My home is	huge. quite big. tiny.	4 It hasn't got	electricity. central heating. a garden.

c Make four true statements and one false statement about your home. Tell your partner. Can your partner guess which statement is false?

3 *Language focus*

have got

a Look at these examples:

1 I*'ve got* two brothers and two sisters.
2 I *haven't got* a garden.
3 How many bedrooms *has* it *got*?
4 It *hasn't got* any electricity.

b Put the correct form of *have got* in these sentences.

1 Our house __ three bedrooms.
2 I __ a brother and two sisters.
3 __ you __ your own flat? — Yes, I have.
4 We __n't __ a garden, but we __ two large balconies.
5 How many children __ they __ ? — They __n't __ any.

what . . . like?

a Look at this question and answer.

What's your flat *like*? — It's in a modern block. It's small and it's got one room and a kitchen.

b Find out as much as you can about your partner's town/home/family. Ask questions using *have got* and *what . . . like*?

Example *What's* your town *like*?
Have you *got* any sisters/children?
What's she *like*?/*What* are they *like*?

4 *Home in a barrel*

a **Read the article quickly and answer the questions.**

1 What does Roger do?
2 Where does Roger live?
3 What is his home like?

b **Write two lists about what Roger a) has got b) hasn't got in his home. Tell your partner.**

Example He's got a comfortable living room.

c **What do you like/dislike about Roger's house? Tell the class.**

AMERICAN PROFESSOR, Roger Doudna, lives in a barrel. The barrel is, in fact, an old whisky vat. It is made of wood and is about 6 metres across and 2.5 metres high. Roger made his home comfortable with the help of an architect. Windows and doors are cut out of the sides, and inside the barrel there is a comfortable living room, a kitchen and a bathroom. There is no bedroom, but there is a ladder leading up to a large platform where he sleeps. He hasn't got much furniture - and it's certainly not expensive: a second-hand sofa and armchairs are covered with rugs, and his coffee table is made from a large piece of wood on logs. 'People lived in circles before they lived in boxes,' says Roger

5 *Designs on a room*

a **Listen to an interior designer describing one of these bedrooms. Which one is she describing? Which one do you prefer? Why?**

b **Now look at the plan of one of the bedrooms in part a. Which one is it?**
***Student A*: Describe bedroom B.**
***Student B*: Draw a plan of bedroom B, without looking at the picture.**

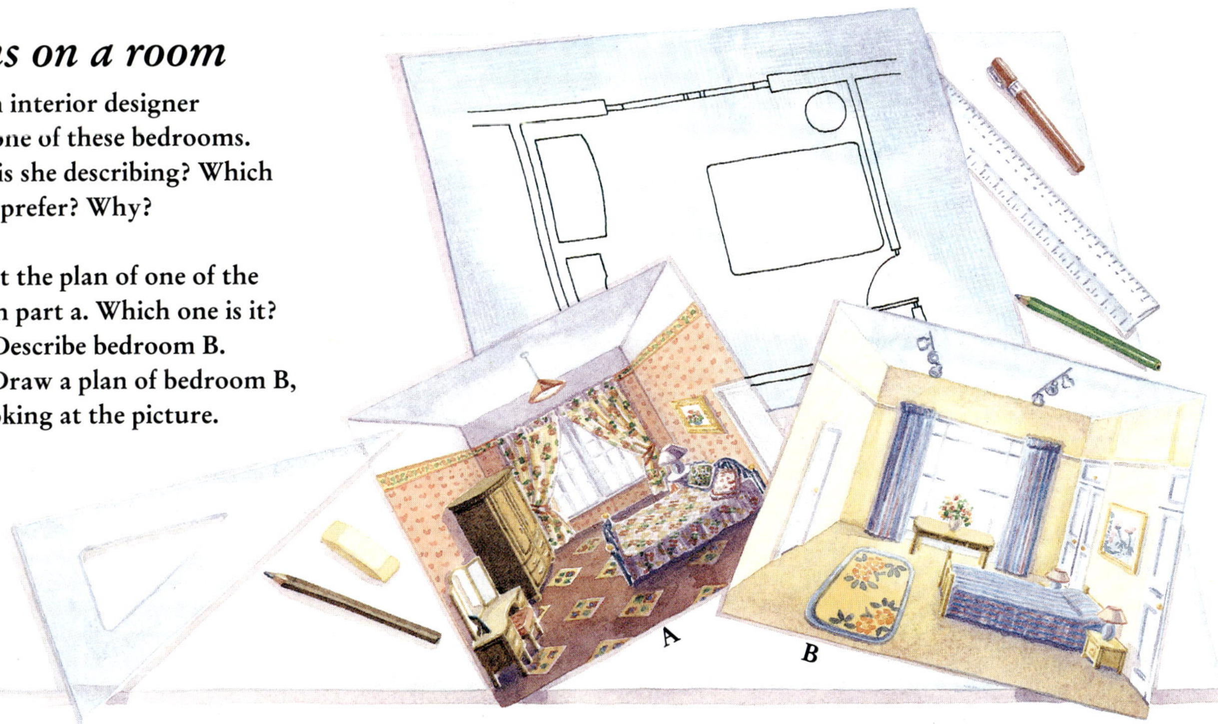

6 *Vocabulary*

Look at the family tree. Write five sentences about the relationships between the members of the family.

Example Philip is Peter's grandfather.

father mother grandfather
nephew niece cousin
brother sister son daughter
husband wife grandmother

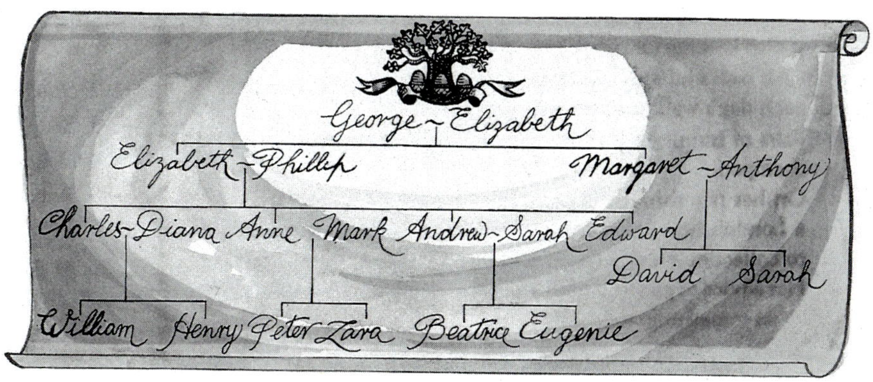

UNIT 3

Fancy that!

1 Saying what you think

a **What are your ambitions for the future?**
Think about: work, study, health, travel, marriage, home.

b **Now ask and answer questions in pairs like this:**

Have you got any ambitions for the future?
Do you want to . . . ? — I want to/don't want to . . .

2 African walk

a **Read the text quickly and answer the questions.**

1 What is Ffyona Campbell's ambition?
2 What is she doing in London at present?

b **Read the text again and answer these questions.**

1 What preparations is Ffyona making for her walk?
2 Write down all the numbers you can find in the text and then tell your partner what these numbers mean. E.g. 24 = She is 24 years old.
3 Would you like to go on a journey like this? Why?/ Why not?

Twenty-four-year-old Ffyona Campbell has a very clear ambition. She wants to walk the length of Africa - a distance of 14,000 km. She plans to spend 13 months on the journey - walking about 40 km per day.

Ffyona's ambition is not impossible. At 16, she walked the length of Britain, at 18, she walked across the USA and now she is writing a book, 'Feet of Clay' about her long journey across Australia two years ago.

At the moment she is in London collecting money for her African adventure. So far she has collected £50,000. She has bought a Land Rover and is now looking for two drivers. She is fitting the Land Rover with beds and a shower. She wants to be comfortable after each day's walk, so she is buying everything she needs: 30 pairs of training shoes, 60 pairs of socks and 50 bottles of shampoo.

On her trip through Britain, Ffyona collected £25,000 for a London hospital. On her African expedition, she wants to collect much more money - for an international charity. Her advice to people with big ambitions is, 'If you really want to do something, then don't be afraid to do it.'

3 Language focus

present continuous

a **Look at this example:**

She *is collecting* money for her African walk.

is collecting **is in the present continuous. Does this mean a) 'now', b) 'always' or c) 'in the future'?**

b **Find other examples of the present continuous from the text and write them down.**

want + *to* + infinitive

a **Look at this example:**

She *wants to walk* the length of Africa.

Find more examples in the text of ***want*** **+** ***to*** **+ infinitive and write them down. This verb is not usually used in the continuous form.**

b **Complete the sentences using the present simple or the present continuous of the verbs in brackets.**

1 Ffyona (*look for*) two drivers to go with her.
2 She (*want/find*) experienced drivers.
3 She (*write*) a book about her walk across Australia.
4 When you (*want/complete*) your journey?
5 What you (*do*) at the moment?
6 I (*prepare*) everything for the journey and I (*collect*) as much money as I can.

4 *Dreams come true*

a Listen to the radio phone-in programme and answer the questions.

1 How many people phone in?
2 What are their ambitions?
to learn Chinese   to visit Hong Kong   to learn to fly
to run a Marathon   to pass a driving test
3 What are they doing to make their dreams come true?
running 20 miles a day   studying hard   working in a factory
having lessons every day   packing boxes   eating a lot

b Listen again, and say if these statements are true or false. Correct the false statements.

1 Sue wants to get a job in a factory.
2 She is saving money.
3 She has got her ticket.
4 Alan wants to run in the Tokyo Marathon.
5 Matthew is trying to pass his driving test.
6 He needs to drive for his job.

5 *My way*

On a piece of paper, write one of your ambitions and say what you are doing to make your ambition possible. Give your paper to another person. In groups discuss which ambition is a) possible b) impossible.

6 *A driving ambition*

a Listen to Sarah Jones calling a driving school and talking to the receptionist. Notice how they ask for and give information. Complete the sentences below.

1 How __ __ each lesson __ ?
2 __ __ book the test lesson __ ?
3 __ __ next Wednesday __ __ __ ?
4 __ __ your name and address __ ?

b Have a similar conversation with your partner about one of the following.

a language lesson   a sports/dancing lesson   a music lesson.

OPERATION RALEIGH is an international —[1] which works with —[2] between the ages of 17 and 25. It organises —[3] all over the world. Members of these expeditions are of many —[4]. Each expedition lasts about 3 —[5] and members have the opportunity to —[6] to distant —[7] and work together on conservation and community projects.

7 *Vocabulary*

Look at the short text about Operation Raleigh — a charity that helps ambitions come true — and fill in the gaps using these words.

months   travel   countries   nationalities   young people   charity   expeditions

UNIT 4

Detective work

1 *Saying what you think*

a **Do you recognise any of the detectives in the photos?**

b **Which of these points do you agree with?**

A good detective needs to:
be intelligent   know the right people
be good at talking to people   be careful   be friendly
be quick-thinking   like danger   be good at paperwork

Sherlock Holmes was born in 1854. He went to Oxford University where he studied science. He was a great reader. He knew a lot about philosophy, politics and literature. Holmes left university and started work as a detective. He became very famous as he solved more and more cases. He met his assistant, Dr John Watson, in 1881 and they later shared rooms at the now famous address of 221B Baker Street, London. However, Dr Watson got married in 1888 and moved out, but he continued to help Holmes with his detective work. Holmes never married. In 1903, Holmes retired to the country where he kept bees and studied their habits. He was only about 50 years old, so why did he retire so early? Perhaps he became a government spy ...

2 *Elementary, my dear Watson!*

a **Read the text about Sherlock Holmes and then choose the correct answer in each case.**

1 At Oxford, Holmes studied a) politics b) science.
2 Holmes a) got married in 1888 b) remained single.
3 People a) know b) don't know why Holmes retired.

b **Now listen to part of a radio programme about Sherlock Holmes and complete the sentences below. What do you think Holmes did?**

1 Perhaps he __ __ and __ to lead a quiet life.
2 I think he __ to __ because he was such an active and energetic person.
3 I don't think he __ __ and I don't think he __ .

3 *Language focus*

simple past

a **Look at these examples:**

1 He was only about 50 years old.
2 He met his assistant in 1881.

Find the simple past verbs in the two sentences.

b **Look at the text in exercise 2 and find other examples of verbs in the simple past. Write them down.**

c **Complete this chart about Sherlock Holmes.**

Verb	Information
(Holmes) . . .	in 1854
(He) . . .	to Oxford University
(He) . . .	a great reader
(He) knew	. . .
(Holmes) . . .	university
(He) started	. . .
(Holmes) met	. . .
(They) . . .	rooms at 221B Baker Street
(Dr Watson) . . .	in 1888
(Watson) continued	. . .
(Holmes) retired	. . .
(He) . . .	only about 50

In pairs, tell his story in your own words. Use the information in the chart to help you.

4 *The Woman in Black*

a This is the strange story of a man arrested for murder and then freed the next day. The paragraphs are jumbled. Put them into the correct order.

b In groups, try to find the explanation for this story. Only one student, Student A, can read the tapescript at the back of the book. Other students ask questions to find the answers.

Example Was the woman dead? Did the man murder the woman? Did she know him?

Student A can only answer 'Yes', 'No' or 'I don't know'.

c Now listen to the tape to find the solution.

1 There was a story in the newspapers the next day about a man arrested for murder at a railway station near Vienna. The papers said the police kept the man for a few hours but then released him. He was a free man.

....

2 The man and the woman did not speak and the woman did not look at the man. She was wearing a black hat with a veil over her face, and a pair of black gloves. After a few minutes the woman took off her gloves. When the man saw her hands he went very pale. He jumped up and put his hands around the woman's throat.

....

3 In 1949 a man got on a train going to Vienna. His clothes were very old fashioned, they looked about 20 years out of date. He went into a compartment where there was nobody except a woman of about his age.

....

4 When the train arrived at the next station, the police were on the platform. The guard and the train driver handed the man over to the police and some of the passengers carried the woman off the train. The police arrested the man immediately and he went quietly with the police, without protesting.

5 *Test your skills*

a Are you a good detective? Look at picture A for 30 seconds and try to remember where everything is.

b Now cover picture A and look at picture B. Tell your partner what is different like this:

In A the newspaper was on the table. In B it's on the floor.

A

B

6 *Vocabulary*

Complete the phrases in the illustrations with the correct word from the list.

murder pickpockets kidnapped hijackers vandalism

UNIT 5

Eating for health

1 *Saying what you think*

a In pairs, discuss which of the statements you think are true.

1 Chocolate gives you spots.
2 Bananas give you energy.
3 Carrots help you to see in the dark.
4 Rice makes you fat.
5 The healthiest diet is a vegetarian diet.

b Give reasons why you think the statements are true or false.

2 *Health break*

a Read the headline. What do you think the article is about? Can you think of ten words which are probably in it? Now read the article and see how many of your words you can find.

b Write a list of Karen's bad habits before she went to Haven Health Farm. Do you have these, or other, bad habits?

c Which paragraphs are about a) Karen's new habits b) general teenage health problems c) the health farm's results d) Karen's old habits?

DOWN ON THE HEALTH FARM

1 'THOUSANDS OF TEENAGERS ARE OVERWEIGHT,' says Haven Health Farm manager, Lorraine Fyne. The staff at the Health Farm say that many teenagers often do not know how to eat well and stay healthy, like Karen.

2 Karen Potter was 13 years old. She weighed 110 kilos and was 1.55m tall. Karen usually had a large bowl of cereal, with a few spoons of sugar, for breakfast. After her cereal, she often ate the left-over food from the night before. At school, she always bought a chocolate bar at break time and every lunch time she had fried chicken and chips. In the evening, Karen usually had more fried food and she often ate a packet of biscuits or a box of chocolates in front of the television. She sometimes went out for a take-away Chinese meal or pizza before going to bed. Karen never ate any fruit and she rarely had fresh vegetables. Her main exercise was changing the TV channel or opening the fridge door.

3 Haven Health Farm helped Karen with her diet and exercise plan. She now eats lots of fresh fruit and vegetables and goes swimming regularly - she never did any sport before because she was always so embarrassed about her size. She now weighs 60 kilos and is still losing weight.

4 Lorraine Fyne says, 'Teenagers often come to the Farm depressed and with very little confidence. When they leave us they are usually happier and much more confident about themselves.'

3 *Health check*

Are the students in the class interested in healthy living? Complete the questionnaire to find out.
Ask several students the questions and record their answers. Tell the class the results.

1	Do you have breakfast?	ALWAYS	USUALLY	SOMETIMES	NEVER
2	Are you careful about what you eat and drink?	ALWAYS	USUALLY	SOMETIMES	NEVER
3	How often do you weigh yourself?	EVERY DAY	ONCE A WEEK	FROM TIME TO TIME	NEVER
4	How often do you exercise?	EVERY DAY	ONCE A WEEK	FROM TIME TO TIME	NEVER

4 *Language focus*

adverbs of frequency

a **Look at these examples:**

1 She *never* did any sport before.
2 She was *always* so embarrassed about her size.

What is the position of the adverb in a) sentence 1 and b) sentence 2?
Complete the rules about adverbs of frequency.

With the verb *to be*, the adverb of frequency comes . . . With other verbs, it comes . . .

b **These are adverbs of frequency: *always, never, often, rarely, sometimes, usually*. Copy this table and put each adverb into the correct place.**

0%	10%	35%	65%	80%	100%
never					

Look at the text in exercise 2 and find sentences with adverbs of frequency.

c **Put the adverbs in brackets in to the correct place in the sentence.**

1 Overweight teenagers eat the wrong kind of food. (*usually*)
2 They are depressed about their weight. (*often*)
3 They eat fresh fruit and vegetables. (*rarely*)
4 Karen ate fruit when she was younger. (*never*)
5 She bought chocolate at break time. (*always*)
6 Do you eat the wrong kind of food? (*sometimes*)

5 *A dancer's diet*

a **Which of these foods do you think a dancer eats?**

bread butter potatoes milk fish steak chicken cheese chips pasta rice raw vegetables

b **Now listen to Gill and see if you were right.**

c **Listen again and say if these statements are true or false. Correct the false statements.**

Example Gill is an amateur dancer.
No, she isn't. She is a professional dancer.

1 Gill is very careful about what she eats.
2 She never has breakfast.
3 She usually has a small lunch.
4 She rarely eats steak.

6 *Offering food and drink*

a **Listen to the first conversation, and choose the best answer.**

1 They are at a a) night club b) health club c) party.
2 The man has a) beer b) carrot juice c) orange juice.
3 He also wants some a) ice b) water c) food.

b **Now listen to the second conversation and choose the best answer.**

1 They are at a a) restaurant b) self-service cafe c) friend's house.
2 The woman has a) cola b) tea c) coffee.
3 The man has tea with a) lemon b) milk and sugar c) milk and no sugar.

c **Listen to both conversations again and complete the sentences.**

1 **offering:** __ __ a drink?
__ __ or coffee, madam?
2 **accepting:** __ __, I'll have a beer.
__ __ coffee, please.
3 **refusing:** __, __ just __, __.

7 *Vocabulary*

a **In pairs, look at the menus and ask for the meanings of any words you don't know.**

b ***Student A*: order a meal. *Student B*: take student A's order and suggest alternatives.**

UNIT 6

What a job!

1 *Saying what you think*

a Look at the photographs and say what jobs you think the people do.

Example What do you think she/he does?
— I think she/he is a/an ...
— Perhaps she/he . . .

b Now check with other students. Have you got the same answers?

2 *Army life*

a Read the text. Do you think it is from a) a newspaper article or b) an army information booklet? Give your reasons.

b Now answer these questions.

1 What does Catherine like about her job?
2 Would you like this job? Why?/Why not?
3 Do you think it is a good idea to have women soldiers?

c In pairs, make two lists of the good and bad points about being a professional soldier.

CAPTAIN CATHERINE JONES

'I was always very keen on sport at school but I didn't know which career I wanted. I liked being outdoors and I wanted to travel. I thought about going to university but I wasn't sure - I didn't like being dependent on my parents. So, I asked a few people: 'What's it like in the army?' And everyone told me: 'Too hard for a girl,' so I applied! After my basic training, I became Commander of a group of 16-year-old recruits - it was very hard at first, but I enjoyed teaching them and helping them through their first few weeks. I think it was an advantage being a woman because, in the end, they talked to me about their problems in a more open way than to their male officers. My first job abroad was in Australia, which was a great experience. I loved travelling around Australia and I enjoyed learning how another army worked. Since I joined the army, I have become more confident and self-disciplined.

Are you flexible and open-minded? Do you like meeting different types of people? Do you like working hard? Do you enjoy learning new things every day?

THEN, MAYBE THE ARMY IS FOR YOU!

3 *Language focus*

love, like, enjoy, didn't like + ing

a Complete the sentences with words from the text in exercise 2.

1 I like __ outdoors.
2 I didn't like __ dependent on my parents.
3 I enjoyed __ them and __ them with their problems.
4 I loved __ around Australia.
5 Do you like __ hard?

What do you notice about each word after *like, enjoy* and *love*? These words are called 'gerunds'.

b Find more sentences in the text with the verbs like, *enjoy* and *love*. Write them down and underline the gerund in each sentence.

too and *very*

a Look at these examples:

1 It's *too* hard for a girl.
2 It was *very* hard at first.

Too is only used for a negative meaning.

Example *Too* hard = It's so hard that you don't want to/can't do it.

b Complete these sentences with *too* or *very.*

1 I don't want to join the army. It's __ dangerous.
2 My training was __ hard, but I enjoyed it.
3 Australia is a __ interesting country.
4 I think travelling to different countries is __ exciting, but Australia is __ far away.

4 *Position vacant*

a Look at the job advertisements and listen to the tape. Which ones do the speakers ask questions about?

b Listen again. Notice how the speakers ask for and give explanations. Complete the sentences below.

1 ___ ___ 'experienced' ___?
2 ___ ___ they have done the job before.
3 ___ ___ explain the ___ of 'qualifications'?
4 ___ the ___ ___ 'exams' or 'diplomas'.

c Use your phrases from part b to ask for the meaning of any words you do not know. Ask the class. Also use the phrases to give any explanations you can.

1

WANTED
Experienced cook for touring circus.
Must love cooking, travelling, people and animals
Apply box 18.

2

ASSISTANT NEEDED in Kenyan Safari Park. Must have relevant science qualifications, and a love of animals is essential.
Contact box 62.

3

WANTED TEMPORARY ASSISTANT TO ZOO-KEEPER
Strong, hard-working young person needed for summer.
Must have a driving licence.
Apply box 20

4

Position vacant for Tour Guide in Europe.
Must be good at languages and enjoy travelling.
No qualifications necessary.
APPLY BOX 201.

1	DO YOU LIKE TRAVELLING? ☐ YES ☐ NO ☐ NOT SURE
2	DO YOU ENJOY WORKING WITH CHILDREN? ☐ YES ☐ NO ☐ DON'T MIND
3	DO YOU ENJOY WORKING WITH ANIMALS? ☐ YES ☐ NO ☐ NOT SURE
4	HAVE YOU GOT A CLEAN DRIVING LICENCE? ☐ YES ☐ NO

5 *Right for the job?*

a In pairs, read the questions in the survey. Write more questions for the jobs in exercise 4.

b Then ask and answer the questions in pairs. Write down your partner's answers. Which of the five jobs do you think a) she/he could do b) you could do? Give your reasons.

6 *Unusual jobs*

a Listen to the two people talking about their jobs. What do they do?

b Listen again and answer these questions.

1 What do they like and dislike about their jobs?
– doing the same thing every day
– waiting for the phone to ring
– working hard then having a few days off
– bad weather
– dancing
– talking to people

2 Why do you think Andrew's job is more popular with women than men?
3 Do you think Jason's job is a good way to earn a living?
4 Would you like to do either of these jobs?

We need **young, enthusiastic sales** –¹ for new sales team. No –² or –³ necessary as we give full training on the job. Must have clean driving –⁴. –⁵ not important, but prefer between 20 and 40. We prefer people who can speak one or more foreign –⁶. We offer: a busy, friendly atmosphere, good –⁷ - about £20,000 p.a., good –⁸ - 6 weeks per year. Company car included.

7 *Vocabulary*

a Put these words into the correct place in the job advertisement.

age experience holidays languages licence qualifications salary staff

b In pairs, write a similar advertisement for your job, or a job you would like to do.

You can do it!

1 *Saying what you think*

a How many ways of communicating can you find in the picture? Can you read and/or understand any of them?

b What can other students do?

Example ... can/can't read music.

2 *Universal language*

a Read the newspaper article to find out what Mr Zavalani has done and why.

b Now answer these questions in pairs.

1 What do these numbers from the text stand for?
50 30 600 30 300 a million

2 What do you think are the advantages/disadvantages of Mr Zavalani's system?

3 Do you think it is useful/possible to have a universal language? Tell your partner and then ask another pair what they think.

FIFTY YEARS AGO, TOMOR SALI ZAVALANI emigrated from Albania to the United States of America. 'But,' he says, 'I couldn't find a job because I couldn't speak much English.' Tomor realised that there were a lot of people, like him, who needed to learn a foreign language in a short time. He decided the answer was a universal language. He knew the travel business used symbols for hotel facilities - could he perhaps use this idea to write a language?

He spent 30 years writing a simple language of pictographs or symbols. His language, Jet Era Glyphs, now has 600 symbols. It includes some small signs to show, for example, verb tenses such as past, present or future. Mr Zavalani says, 'Anyone can learn my language in 30 hours.' He would like to teach his language to groups of school children and to people who cannot speak. He says, 'Why can't teachers teach my system in school so that American children can communicate with others across the world?'.

Over the last 300 years, many people have tried to write a universal language. The most famous is Esperanto, written in 1887, which now has a million speakers worldwide. But many experts think that Mr Zavalani is too late - the future of international languages is with the computer, not pen and paper, they say. This is an example of the Jet Era Glyph system.

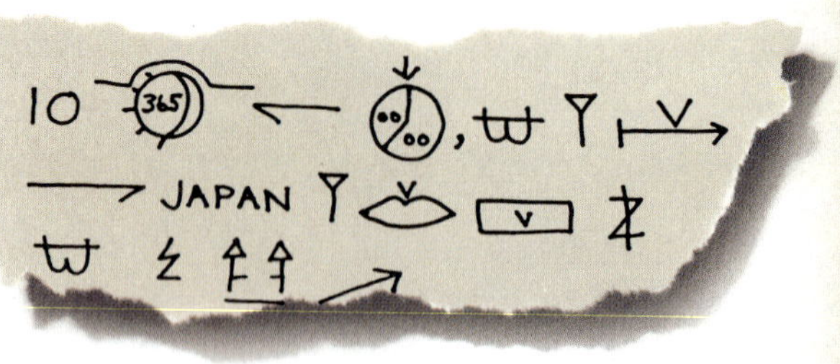

Translation: Ten years from now, when you go to Japan, you will speak in pictograms with the people there.

3 *Language focus*
can/could for ability

a **Look at these examples:**

1 They *can* communicate with other children across the world.
2 I *couldn't* speak much English.

Can **and** ***could*** **do not need** ***do/does/did*** **for questions and negatives.**

b **Find more examples of sentences with** ***can*** **and** ***could*** **in the text in exercise 2. Write them down.**

c **The words of these sentences are jumbled. Put the words into the correct order.**

1 speak/when/child/you/were/a/could/English/you?
2 you/languages/many/can/how/speak?
3 could/Mr Zavalani/speak/find/not/a/because/could/he/job/English/not.
4 people/Esperanto/many/can/speak/how?
5 by/can/translate/computers/we/everything/not.

d **Find out what your partner can do now and if she/he could do these things as a child.**

Example *Can* you swim/drive/ski/speak French/type/stand on your hands/run a kilometer?
Could you swim when you were a child?

How many things can/can't your partner do now that she/he couldn't/could do as a child?

4 *Writing in pictographs*

a **Look back at the Jet Era Glyph sentence in exercise 2. In pairs, work out what each of the symbols means.**

Example

= year

= plural

b **Now make up some symbols for your own pictograph language.**

Write them down and give them to another pair. They write a sentence in your language. Can you understand your own language?

5 *Can you read Japanese?*

a **Listen to Hiro talking about learning to read and write in Japanese and answer the questions.**

1 Why is learning to read and write difficult?
2 Why do children learn Hiragana first?

b **Are these statements true or false? Correct the false statements.**

1 There are five or six thousand characters in the Japanese language.
2 You need to learn two thousand characters before you can read anything.
3 Japanese children cannot read books before they are 14 years old.
4 About two thousand years ago, Japanese people could not read or write their language.
5 All Japanese people can speak Chinese.

6 *Code cracking*

a **In pairs, look at the puzzle. Can you crack the code?**

2426 1302 1206 2312 0719 1808 1106 0101 1522

b **Now listen to two people trying to crack the code. Did you you get it right?**

c **Now listen again and notice how they make suggestions and say they are wrong. Complete the sentences.**

1 __ __ that.
2 That __ __ __.
3 __ __ __ try it backwards?

7 *Vocabulary*

a **Can you understand the symbols? Write down their meaning.**

b **In pairs, say a) what the hotel has/hasn't got, b) what you can/can't do in the hotel.**

UNIT 8

Twenties' fever

1 *Saying what you think*

a Look at the pictures of famous people in the 1920s. Do you know why they were famous?

b What can you say about the differences in style between the twenties and today?

2 *The greatest escapologist*

a Look at the photograph of Harry Houdini. What do you think he was famous for? Read the text to find out if you were right.

b Read the text again and answer the questions.

1 What was Houdini's real name?
2 What jobs did he have?
3 What tricks did he do?

Harry Houdini lived from 1874 to 1926. His real name was not Houdini but Ehrich Weiss. He was born in Budapest, Hungary but his family emigrated to the United States of America when he was a boy. He joined a circus as a trapeze artist when he was still a child but it was not in the circus that he became famous.
In his teens, he began to do magic tricks and he changed his name to Harry Houdini. He took his stage name from a famous French magician of the 19th century, Jean Robert-Houdin. At first, he worked in small theatres around the USA as a magician. He did not become famous immediately. But then in the 1920s, he began to do escaping tricks. People tied his arms and legs in chains, they locked him in prison cells and he always escaped. Once they put him into a large wooden box, tied the box with chains and threw him into a river but he still escaped. How did he escape? No-one ever knew. Was he the greatest escapologist of all time? Even today, many people think he was. Houdini did not die from his dangerous tricks but from a stomach disease in 1926 .

Harry Handcuff Houdini.

3 *Language focus*

past simple negatives and questions

a Look at these questions:

1 *Was* he the greatest escapologist of all time?
2 *How* did he escape?

You need to use *did* for questions in the past except with the verb *to be*.

b Match the questions in A with the answers in B.

A

1 When did his family emigrate to the USA?
2 When did he begin to do escaping tricks?
3 When was he born?
4 Did he die because of his magic tricks?
5 Was he born in the USA?
6 When did he die?
7 Did he work in a circus?

B

a In 1874.
b In 1926.
c No, he wasn't, he was born in Hungary.
d When he was a boy.
e Yes he did. He was a trapeze artist.
f In the 1920's.
g No he didn't, he died from a stomach disease.

4 *Comic hero*

Look at the notes about the life of Charlie Chaplin. Write down his life story from the notes.

Born: *1889, London, a poor family.*

First job: *actor in London theatres.*

In USA: *from 1910 to 1952, never became US citizen.*

First film: *1914, as a tramp - old clothes, trousers too big, shoes too big, coat too small, carried a walking stick - very successful.*

Film career: *1918 started his own film company, directed films, wrote music for films. Last film in 1952.*

Personal life: *5 wives. 1952 travelled to Europe, American government said he was a communist, never went back to live in USA. Lived in Switzerland from 1952 - till he died on December 25th 1977.*

A

B

1 **1927:** The first film with sound arrived. It was called The Jazz Singer. Mickey Mouse made his first appearance in a cartoon film. On May 31st, Charles Lindbergh flew non-stop from New York to Paris.

2 **1922:** Howard Carter found the 3,000-year-old tomb of the Egyptian King, Tutenkhamun, in Luxor, Egypt. There were boxes of gold, hundreds of jewels and a beautiful golden mask.

3 **1929:** On October 24th, the American financial market in Wall Street collapsed. Thousands of businesses closed. Hundreds of thousands of people lost their jobs in the USA and all over Europe.

4 **1920s:** During this decade women's dresses got much shorter, women started to smoke in public and everyone tried the new dance - the Charleston.

5 **1926 :** The first TV set appeared.

C

5 *The roaring twenties*

a Listen to this man talking about his memories of the 1920s in the USA. Which of the news stories in the photographs does he mention?

b Listen again and say if the sentences are true or false. Correct the false sentences.

1 The first TV came out in the 1920s.
2 Nobody had a car in the USA before 1920.
3 His family bought their first washing machine at this time.
4 Everyone in the States was rich in the 1920s.
5 The financial market collapsed in 1929.
6 His family did not lose much money in the Wall Street Crash.
7 By 1930, millions of Americans did not have a job.

6 *1920s news sheet*

a Read the short articles about famous events of the 1920s. Match the photographs with three of the events.

b Put each of the news events under one of these headings.

entertainment economics fashion transport ancient history disaster

7 *Vocabulary*

Match the phrases in column A with those in column B.

Example In the nineteenth century = 1889

A	B
1 In this decade.	a 1889
2 In the next century.	b 23 years old
3 In the nineteenth century.	c 1927
4 In his twenties.	d 1994
5 In the nineteen fifties.	e 15 years old
6 In the last decade.	f 2006
7 In the nineteen twenties.	g 1956
8 In her teens.	h 1987

UNIT 9

Are you green?

1 *Saying what you think*

a **Can you find these types of pollution in the pictures? Which one do you think is the most dangerous?**

litter   traffic   factory waste   noise

b **Do you think people talk too much about the environment?**

2 *What can you do?*

a **Read the leaflet which tells us what we can do to help our environment. Put the verb in brackets into the correct form, either positive or negative.**

Example Don't buy food in plastic containers.

b **Answer the questions.**

1 Do you follow some of these rules? Which ones?
2 Can you suggest any more rules to add to the leaflet?
3 Do you agree with all/some of the rules?

(Buy/Don't buy) food in plastic containers.

(Teach/Don't teach) your children about healthy eating.

When possible, **(travel/don't travel)** by public transport.

(Take/Don't take) the car if you can walk or cycle.

If you drive, **(use/don't use)** unleaded petrol and **(get/don't get)** a car which uses a lot of petrol per kilometre.

(Switch off/Don't switch off) electric lights when you are not using them.

Instead of turning up the heating in the house, **(put on/don't put on)** a sweater.

(Wear/Don't wear) fur coats.

When you buy writing paper, **(look for/don't look for)** recycled paper.

(Throw/Don't throw) litter in the street; **(take/don't take)** it home with you or **(use/don't use)** a litter bin.

3 *Green maze*

a This maze has three exits. In pairs find the exit to green fields.

b Listen to two rubbish collectors, Speaker A and Speaker B. Which one leads you to the rubbish and which one to the glass?

c Listen again. Who says these phrases?

1 Turn right after the statue.
2 Take the third turning on the right.
3 Turn left before the fountain.
4 Take the second turning on the left.

d Choose one of the paths and explain the directions to your partner, from the entrance to the exit. Use the phrases above to help you.

4 *Language focus*

the imperative

a Look at these examples:

1 Don't throw litter in the street.
2 Take it home with you.

Find the verb in each sentence. They are both in the imperative form. Which one is a) positive b) negative?

b Choose the correct verbs from this list to complete the text about cycling. Put the verb into the correct form, positive or negative.

be forget go save spend take wear waste

If you are going on a short journey, __¹ your car; __² by bike. __³ money on petrol - __⁴ money and energy! __⁵ your time in a traffic jam. Get to your destination quicker and cheaper by cycling. But remember, __⁶ careful. If you cycle at night __⁷ brightly coloured clothes and __⁸ to switch on your lights.

5 *Right or wrong?*

a Read the two short articles, then listen to the three conversations. Which conversation is about a) article 1 b) article 2 c) neither of the articles?

1 Beetle fighting is popular in some parts of Thailand. People organise fights between beetles, for money. These fighting beetles are usually 5cm long and black.

2 Disposable nappies cost £500 a year per baby. Each baby needs about five trees per year for the paper in throw-away nappies. Used nappies stay on the Earth for thousands of years because the outside is made of plastic.

b Listen again and notice how the speakers ask for opinions and agree and disagree. Complete the sentences.

1 What __ __ __ about using animals for sport?
2 I __ __ with it. It's __ .
3 Yes, that's __, I __ .

c Do you agree/disagree with any of the speakers?

6 *Vocabulary*

a Which words have a similar meaning?

aerosols dirty fuel litter petrol polluted rubbish sprays waste

b Can you understand these signs? Where do you think you could see them?

UNIT 10

Leisure time

1 *Saying what you think*

a Look at the pictures of people in their leisure time. Can you name all the activities?

Example Going to the cinema.

Are you interested in these/other leisure activities? Ask your partner, like this:

What do you do in your free time?

b Do you think these statements are true or false for your country?

People aged between 16 and 34 watch 20 hours of television a week.
Over 1.5 million people go to football matches every week.
10% of the population goes to the cinema at least once a month.
Men have more leisure time than women.

HOW ABOUT A WEEKEND WITH A DIFFERENCE? At Quality Hotel you can be a real detective in a MURDER WEEKEND. Can you find the killer? Was it the jealous husband, the niece who needed the money, the family doctor - was it you? Every week, we have a new story and a new mystery for you to solve. Actors mix with the hotel guests but you don't know who they are. So don't trust anyone - the man with the wonderful smile could be the murderer. Be careful what you say and keep your eyes and ears open. **By the end of Saturday evening there is going to be a murder. The question is - when and who?** We begin Friday evening, after dinner. The price includes two nights at the hotel, Saturday and Sunday breakfast and Saturday lunch. Every Saturday evening there is a fancy dress party and dance. You can bring your own fancy dress or hire it from us.
We regret that children under 16 are not allowed.

PRICES PER PERSON FOR THE WEEKEND:
Double room £155, single room £179 (rooms with balcony £10 extra)
All rooms have private bath/shower, colour TV, phone and radio.
Friday evening dinner £12. Hire of costume £34. Private taxi service from station £6. Call us on 0800 444444 for further information.

2 *Murder is my hobby*

a Read the text quickly and answer the questions.

1 Is it a) a newspaper article b) an advertisement? Give reasons for your answer.
2 What is special about a weekend at this hotel?

b Read the text again and answer the questions.

1 What is the hotel called?
2 When does the MurderWeekend begin and end?
3 What does the standard price include?
4 Who cannot go on a Murder Weekend?
5 How much does it cost to hire fancy dress?
6 How can you get more information?

3 *Booking a place*

a Listen to the conversation and answer the questions.

1 When does Mrs Valentine want to go on the Murder Weekend?
2 What kind of room does she book?
3 How much is her bill for the weekend?

b Now listen again and complete these sentences by joining phrases from column A and column B.

A	B
1 She is arriving at the hotel	a taxi from the station.
2 She is staying in	b a week on Friday.
3 They are catching	c his own clothes.
4 They are getting	d a fancy dress costume.
5 They are not having	e a double room without a balcony.
6 She is hiring	f dinner on Friday evening.
7 Her husband is bringing	g the 5.30 train from Cardiff.

4 *Language focus*

the present continuous for future arrangements

a **Look at this example:**

She *is arriving* at the hotel a week on Friday.

The verb is in the present continuous. Is she arriving now or in the future? You use the present continuous to talk about fixed plans and arrangements in the future.

b **Find other examples of the present continuous for fixed plans and arrangements in exercise 3. Ask and answer questions with your partner about Mrs Valentine's arrangements, like this:**

Who *is* she *going* with?
Are they *hiring* fancy dress costumes?

5 *Going out*

a **Read the advertisements for different events. Would you like to go to any of them?**

1 **City walk -** Join us for a tour round the historic sights of London. Visit ancient churches, walk down cobbled streets, admire the architecture and shudder at the dungeons. Walk starts 8.30 am Sunday mornings

2 **Royal Opera House,** Covent Garden. **Swan Lake** for three nights only: June 6, 7, 8 at 7.45 pm. Tickets available from the Box Office at £10, £15 and £30.

3 ODEON CINEMA. Now showing: **Women on the Edge of a Nervous Breakdown** (Mujeres al borde de un Ataque de Nervios). Mon - Sat 5 pm and 8 pm. Doors open 4.30 pm and 7.30 pm.

b **Listen to the three conversations of people inviting others to some of these events and answer the questions.**

1 Where do the speakers invite people to go?
2 In which of the conversations do people a) accept b) refuse?
3 What do you think is the relationship between the speakers in each conversation?

c **Listen again and notice how people invite, accept and refuse. Complete the sentences.**

1 __ __ __ to go?
2 Yes, __ __ to.
3 No, __ __ I __. I'm quite __ at the moment.

d **In pairs, invite and accept or refuse, using the advertisements.**

6 *Activity weekends*

a **Loch Fyne Mansion is an activity holiday centre in Scotland. Listen to the three holiday centre guides. Which of these activities do they mention?**

pottery fishing windsurfing
golf tennis painting
parachuting walking drama
dancing sightseeing
parachuting

b **Listen again and complete the chart for each of the three speakers. In pairs, give a report on each of the activities.**

Name of teacher			
Activities			
Day of activities			
Starting times			

c **Which activities would you choose to do?**

7 *Vocabulary*

If today is 8th May, what is or was the date on the following days?

1 The day before yesterday.
2 The day after tomorrow.
3 In three days' time.
4 This time next week.
5 This Saturday.
6 Last Wednesday.
7 Next Tuesday.
8 A week ago.

UNIT 11

My own business

1 *Saying what you think*

a **What do you need to start your own business?**

b **Which of these are a) very important b) quite important c) not so important? Make three lists in pairs.**

a new idea   a lot of money   a good education   hard work
a love of money   a love of success   good luck   a good partner
confidence   good advertising   friends in the right places

TOP MARKS FOR LOCAL YOUTH ENTERPRISE

2 *Youth enterprise*

a **Can you guess what Youth Enterprise is? Listen to Part 1 of the tape and see if you were correct.**

b **What questions would you like to ask the speaker if you were one of the students? Listen to Part 2. Did the students on the tape ask the same questions as you?**

c **Now listen to Part 3. Complete the questions that students ask.**

1 ___ ___ ties did you ___?
2 ___ ___ profit did you ___ ?
3 ___ ___ students were there in the ___?

3 *Language focus*

How much? How many?

a **Look at these examples:**

1 *How many* schools are there in the scheme?
2 *How much* money do we get to start the business?

Look at this list of words. Which words need a) ***How much . . . ?*** **b)** ***How many . . . ?***

advice   books   money   prizes   profit   time
schools   students

b **Make complete sentences with the phrases in part a and the phrases below.**

Example are there in a business team? + How many students = How many students are there in a business team?

1 are there for the best teams?
2 did you sell?
3 do you get to begin the business?
4 can the business advisers give?
5 do we spend on the business project per week?
6 did you make from selling the ties?

4 *The Multicolour Glass Company*

a Look at the photograph of Mandy. What do you think her business is? Read the text quickly to find out.

b Copy and complete the chart for Mandy's business.

type of business:	
experience:	
qualifications:	
money invested:	
funding from:	
main customers:	

c Do you know any other successful business ventures?

WHEN TWENTY-EIGHT-YEAR-OLD Mandy Jones visited a business exhibition two years ago, she found a great business idea. There was a stand at the exhibition which had a lot of unusual coloured glass. Mandy, a graduate in business studies, was bored with her business - a travel agency, so she decided to start making things out of coloured glass. She persuaded a partner to join her and left the travel agency. They had only £3,000 between them but they needed £20,000 to buy the machinery. They asked ten banks to lend them the money but each bank refused. They did not give up. They heard that a large oil company and an insurance company gave loans for new business ideas. They got £5,000 from the oil company and £3,000 from the insurance company. But they still needed another £9,000. They finally persuaded a bank to lend them the rest of the money.

Now the business is two years old and they have plenty of orders. 'We sell to restaurants, hotels and people with large homes,' says Mandy. 'Perhaps we're lucky, but everything is going very well at the moment.'

5 *Discussion*

In groups, decide what each person is good at. Think of two ideas for a business. What could each person do? Tell the class.

6 *Sympathising and congratulating*

a Listen to the four conversations. Which ones are a) good news b) bad news?

b Listen again. Which responses do people make to good and bad news?

oh dear how wonderful I'm very sorry oh no that's fantastic
congratulations well done what a pity

c Listen to people in Part 2 giving their good and bad news. Make a suitable response to each piece of news.

7 *Vocabulary*

a Use these words to complete the sentences below.

cheque cash banker's card notes

b Where do you think you would see these signs?

Marriage

1 *Saying what you think*

a What is happening in all these pictures? What happens at a wedding in your country? Think about:

clothes special traditions where it takes place food presents

b What kind of wedding would you like/did you have?

2 *Weddings in paradise*

a Would you spend a lot of money on your wedding? Why? Why not?

b Below are the first paragraphs of two articles. Which one is from a) a holiday brochure b) a magazine article. How do you know? Read paragraphs a to d and put them into the correct order in the correct article.

1 WHY NOT HAVE A WEDDING TO REMEMBER ALL YOUR LIFE?

We can arrange weddings in paradise with tropical flowers, a gentle ocean breeze, a beautiful blue sea. You can even get married on the beach with the gentle waters of the Caribbean washing your feet.

2 BOB AND CAROL *have decided on something special for their wedding day. They are going to get married on the beautiful island of Phuket off the west coast of Thailand.*

a We can arrange everything for you. The price of the wedding includes the marriage certificate, a wedding cake, a champagne toast, flowers, a photographer and 24 colour photos. For a little extra cost we can make a video of the ceremony.

b 'Unfortunately our friends can't come,' says Carol. 'So the wedding party is going to be very small. We can't really afford to pay for hundreds of people to fly out with us.' 'But we're going to show everyone the video when we get back,' says Bob.

c Or if you really want a 'heavenly' wedding, why not get married with your heads in the clouds. You can have your wedding ceremony in a hot air balloon, flying over Florida.

d 'Our wedding is going to be as romantic as possible,' they say. 'We are going to get married on Patong Beach in traditional Thai dress.' The reception is in the Coral Beach Hotel with full Thai dinner and a traditional wedding cake. How much is all this going to cost? 'About £8,000,' they say. And what about the guests?

c What do you think are the advantages/disadvantages of Bob and Carol's wedding? Would you like a wedding like this?

3 *Language focus*

going to + infinitive for future plans

a Look at these examples:

1 . . . we are *going to show* everyone the video.
2 We are *going to get married* on Patong Beach.

(to be) going to = plan/intend to

b Find more examples of *going to* from the text and write them down.

c Complete these sentences with the correct form of *going to* and the verb in brackets.

1 Carol (wear) traditional Thai dress.
2 They (not invite) many guests.
3 When Bob gets home, he (show) the wedding video to all their friends.
4 How much the wedding (cost)?
5 Bob and Carol (stay) in Thailand for two weeks.
6 I (not have) a wedding like this.

4 *Different traditions*

a Listen to Yasmin talking about her wedding plans. What kind of wedding is it going to be?

b Listen again and answer the questions.

1 Which colours do people wear at Indian weddings?
2 When do they wear white?
3 What are these people going to do:
a) Yasmin's mother? b) Yasmin's friends? c) the bride's parents?

c How is Yasmin's wedding different from weddings in your country?

5 *Opinions*

What do people in the class think about marriage? Ask four students the questions in this survey. Write down the answers.

1 MARRIAGE IS
- a) very important
- b) sometimes important
- c) not necessary

2 THE BEST AGE FOR MARRIAGE IS
- a) under 20
- b) between 20 and 30
- c) over 30

3 IN MARRIAGE THE HUSBAND AND WIFE ARE
- a) always equal
- b) sometimes equal
- c) never equal

4 IT IS BETTER IF THE HUSBAND AND WIFE ARE
- a) the same ages
- b) different ages
- c) it doesn't matter

6 *Do you agree?*

a Listen to the four conversations. Which phrases do they use to agree and disagree?

that's right I don't agree definitely I think so too I don't think so

b In pairs, discuss your answers to the questions in exercise 5. Agree and disagree with your partner. Use the phrases you wrote down.

7 *Vocabulary*

a Look at these advertisements from a magazine and find the abbreviations in them.

b What do you think these abbreviations mean?

1 frm	6 yrs
2 b&w	7 s/a/e
3 pics	8 rd
4 tel	9 inc.
5 hrs	10pm

UNIT 13

Tips for travellers

1 *Saying what you think*

a How many different methods of transport can you find in the picture? How many of these methods have you used?

b How many different objects can you find in the picture? Do you usually take any of these objects with you on holiday?

c What is your favourite type of holiday?

A B C

2 *Experienced travellers*

a Look at the photos. Which one is of a) Japan b) Egypt c) Sweden?

b Now listen to these three conversations about holiday plans. Which conversation is about a) Japan b) Egypt c) Sweden?

c Listen again and answer the questions.

1 Which of the objects in exercise 1 do the speakers mention?
2 What advice did the friends give about:
   a) shopping in Cairo?
   b) eating out in Egypt?
   c) the best time to travel in Sweden?
   d) staying in youth hostels in Sweden?
   e) the best time to travel in Japan?
   f) clothes to take to Japan?
3 If you know any of these three countries, can you give more advice?

3 *Language focus*

must, should, can

a **Look at these examples:**

1 You *must have* a visa.
2 You *should book* in advance.
3 *Can* you *go* inside all the mosques?

You must = It's necessary because of the regulations.
You should = It's better/I advise you.
You can = It is possible/allowed.

b **Complete these sentences about travelling with *must, should* or *can*.**

1 When you enter Canada, you __ show your passport.
2 You __ smoke in an aeroplane when the 'No Smoking' sign is off.
3 When the plane is taking off everyone __ wear a seatbelt.
4 Before you go to Brazil, you __ learn a little Portuguese.
5 All passengers __ have a boarding card before they get on the plane.
6 You __ buy a ticket for all children over two years old but babies under two __ travel free.

4 *Trick cycles*

Read the letter and answer the questions.

1 What did Ivan Sanderson find?
2 Where did he find them?
3 Why did he recommend them?

HERE in Haiiti, I found three old trick cycles. They were from a circus that came to town a few years ago. All three cycles are as good as new. They weigh only 6 kilos each and it is very easy to take them to pieces. When they are in pieces they fit in a small bag about 60 centimetres square. These bikes are very strong and carry quite heavy loads. They can travel fast over any kind of country, if it is not too mountainous. They save me hours of walking and I use them to carry lots of heavy shopping. If you want to, you can carry them on your back very comfortably. All travellers should have one.

IVAN SANDERSON, Haiti, 1937

5 *In my country*

Write some advice for travellers to your country or a country you know. Write about some of these things.

tourist places   shopping   food   language(s)
weather   accommodation   cost of living   clothes

Give your paper to another student. One student reads out your advice to the class, without saying the country. Other students try to guess the country.

6 *Money matters*

a **Listen to these three conversations. Where does each one take place?**

b **Listen again and answer the questions.**

1 What does each customer want to do?
2 Is it possible? If not, why not?

Bureau de Change

	Rates to the £
A. sch	21.35
B. f	62.75
C. $	2.07
Fr. f	10.36
DM	3.05
Dr	338.00
Gld	3.435
L	2205.00
Esc	263.00
Pst	190.50
Kr	10.51
US $	1.825

7 *Vocabulary*

a **Match the currencies with their abbreviations in the chart.**

German marks   Italian lire   Portugese escudos
Greek drachmas   Swedish krona

b **Can you add any more currencies to the list? Can you work out the value of your country's currency with any of the other currencies?**

UNIT 14

Whizz kids

1 *Saying what you think*

a Do you know the people in the pictures? What was their special talent?

b Which statement(s) do you agree with?

1 Some people are born with a special talent.
2 Everyone has a special talent in something.
3 Everyone can learn to be very good at music, sport, art, etc. if they have a good teacher and a lot of lessons.

c Do you have a special talent?

2 *World class*

a Read the article about the musician, Evelyn Glennie, and find out what is unusual about her.

b Now answer these questions.

1 What does Evelyn do?
2 What did she do when she was a) 14 b) 16?
3 Why did the Academy not want to accept her?
4 How long has she been deaf?
5 What has she learned to do to understand people?
6 How does Evelyn 'hear' music?

Twenty-four-year-old Evelyn Glennie is a percussionist. She has played with orchestras all over the world and gives about 90 concerts a year. At 14, she played with the National Youth Orchestra of Scotland and at 16, she applied to join the Royal Academy of Music. At first, the Royal Academy did not want to accept her. The reason was - Evelyn Glennie is completely deaf. She has been deaf since the age of twelve and has learned to lip-read perfectly.
Evelyn says that Beethoven was right when he said that makng music has nothing to do with hearing it. She can feel the music going up and down her body. The Royal Academy finally listened to Evelyn and they were astonished when they heard her play. They accepted her immediately and she became their star pupil. She is now a world class musician. In such a short time Evelyn has done a lot. She has made several records and she has written **'Good Vibrations'**, her autobiography. Evelyn says, 'It has been a wonderful period of my life.' She has learned a lot and is now thinking about what she wants to do next.

3 *Language focus*

present perfect

a Look at these examples:

1 She *has played* with orchestras all over the world.
2 She *has been* deaf since the age of twelve.

Both sentences use the present perfect.
In sentence 1, she *has played* = at no exact time in the past.
In sentence 2, she *has been* = something began in the past and continues until now.

b Here are some more sentences in the present perfect. Which ones refer to a) no exact time in the past b) something which began in the past and continues to the present?

1 Oh, yes. I've heard her record.
2 She has lived in Scotland all her life.
3 Have you ever heard Evelyn play?
4 I have been interested in music for a long time.
5 She has written her autobiography.
6 Many musicians have said she is a great percussionist.

c Look back at the text in exercise 2 and find more examples of the present perfect.

4 *Talented children*

a Look at the two photos of Ricardo and Stephen. What do you think their talents are? Now listen to part of a radio broadcast on talented children. See if you were correct.

b Read these sentences and say if they are from the interview about Ricardo or the interview about Stephen. Then listen again to check your answers.

1 He has drawn very complex buildings.
2 His father has bought him a computer.
3 We have taught him everything we can.
4 He has always been fantastic at it.
5 He has passed exams for sixteen year olds.
6 Experts have looked at them.

c What do you think are the problems of having special talents?

5 *Geniuses?*

a Can you match these descriptions with some of the people in the pictures in exercise 1? Would you like to have the same talents?

b In groups, choose some people who have special talents. Write short descriptions of them and tell the other students.

1 **PELE** scored over 1,200 goals in 18 years of professional football, starting at the age of 16. He won 3 World Cup medals with the Brazilian national team. He retired at 34.

2 **MUHAMMED ALI** was born in 1942. In 1964 he changed his name from Cassius Clay to Muhammed Ali. He was the World Champion in boxing 3 times. He began his professional career in 1960 and retired in 1979.

3 **GRETA GARBO** starred in 31 films. She was the silent movie heroine who stayed famous when talking films arrived. She was a recluse for many years before she died on April 15th 1990.

4 **MOZART** first wrote music when he was six years old. He wrote over 1000 pieces of music during his lifetime. He died in poverty when he was 35.

6 *Checking understanding*

a Listen to the two conversations about Pele and Mozart. In each conversation someone is checking that they understood correctly. Write down the phrases they use to check understanding.

b In pairs, have similar conversations about Muhammed Ali and Greta Garbo.

7 *Vocabulary*

Match the headlines with the stories. How do you think the articles finish?

1 **YOUNG TALENT**

2 **BOY GENIUS**

3 **CHAMPION DEFEATED**

4 **SUPERSTAR TO MARRY**

a **9-YEAR-OLD MARTIN JONES astonished the examiners when he beat the best brains in Britain and achieving 100% in**

b 23-year-old Gloria Trew who started her professional career aged 3 when she starred in 'Heaven on Earth', announced her engagement to actor

c 13-year-old violinist, Susan Brent, won the 'Young Musician of the Year' award yesterday. 'She plays with extraordinary skill', said one judge

d Boxer, ANDY MACDONALD, announced his retirement yesterday after losing his title to

UNIT 15

Two's company

1 *Saying what you think*

a Is anyone in the class Gemini? Is this description true?

b Do you know any real twins? Do they look the same? Do they have similar personalities?

2 *Freaks?*

a **Read this text and answer these questions.**

1 Where is Twinsburg?
2 What is it like?
3 What happens there?

b **Read the text again and compare these things:**

1 The way Chrissie and Cathy feel a) in normal life, and b) inTwinsburg.
2 Twinsburg a) usually, and b) at the time of the festival.
3 The relationship between a) Mark and Mike, and b) other brothers and sisters.
4 The festival a) in 1976, and b) now.

'People often stare at us. We sometimes feel like freaks' said Chrissie and Cathy Wiedenheft. 'It's easier here with 10,000 other twins. We feel at home.' Chrissie and Cathy are spending the weekend in Twinsburg, Ohio, USA. For 362 days a year Twinsburg is a quiet little town. There's a small high street with a MacDonalds and a Pizza Parlour and not much nightlife. But for one weekend every year, it's the centre for twins from around the world. 10,000 twins take part in a big parade through the town - twins on bikes, baby twins in pushchairs, Rock 'n Roll twins, the fattest twins in the world, the oldest twins in the world, punk twins, nun twins. Anybody can come but you must be a twin.

'We think we're closer than other brothers or sisters,' said Mike and Mark Miller. ' If something's wrong with him, I can feel it - so I always phone him,' said Mike. 'Yes,' agreed Mark. 'I think that we have a better relationship than many brothers - except when he steals my girlfriends.' Mike laughed and explained, 'Well, I'm better looking than he is.'

People often stare at us. We sometimes feel like freaks.

The first twin festival at Twinsburg was in 1976 and 72 people came. It cost the organisers £200. Of course, now it is bigger, busier, more famous and more expensive than the first one. Last year's festival was the most expensive. It cost about £50,000. There are now plans to build a Twinsburg museum of the most famous twins in history and a library for the world's biggest collection of information and data about twins.

3 *Language focus*

comparatives and superlatives

a **Look at this example:**

Now it is *bigger*, *busier* and *more expensive* than the first time.

The adjectives *big*, *busy* and *expensive* change to *bigger*, *busier* and *more expensive* when they are used in the 'comparative' form.

How do the spellings change?

Do you know when to use *-er* and when to use *more*?

Which word comes after the comparative form?

b **Can you find more examples of the comparative form in the text?**

What is the comparative form of the word *good*?

c **Look at this example:**

. . . the *fattest* twins in the world . . .

The adjective *fat* changes to *fattest* in the 'superlative' form.

Can you find other examples of the superlative form in the text?

When do you use *-est* and when do you use *most*?

d **Look at the things you compared in exercise 2. Make sentences about the things you compared using comparative forms.**

Example The Twinsburg festival is *busier* than usual.

e **What can you say about Twinsburg using the superlative form?**

Example In Twinsburg you can see the *fattest* twins in the world.

4 *Identical twins*

a **Do twins usually have a special relationship? Do you know any unusual stories about twins?**

b **Listen to this interview and answer the questions.**

1 What does *identical* mean?
2 What 'trick' did the twins play on their teachers?
3 How are Peter and Martin different?
4 What was unusual about the language they spoke?
5 What did they mean when they said *Gobu* and *Tek*?

5 *Multiple births*

a **Put these adjectives into the superlative form and then put them into the correct place in the text.**

heavy unusual high short

1 **The ...... number of babies born at one birth is 9.** But not all these babies survived. The highest number of surviving babies is 6. Mrs Rosanna Gianni had 4 boys and 3 girls on January 11th 1980 in Florence, Italy.

2 **The ...... twins in the world were Billy and Benny McCrary** from North Carolina, USA. They weighed 337kg and 328kg.

3 **The ...... twins in the world were Matjus and Bela Matina,** born in 1903 in Budapest, Hungary. As adults they measured 76cm.

4 **The ...... twins are 'Siamese' twins. Nadir and Juraci Climerio de Oliverra,** born in Brazil in 1957, were joined at the body. Their body had two heads, four arms and two legs.

b **Can you find the answer to this puzzle?**

There was a murder in a New York street. Lots of people saw the crime and the murderer. The police arrested the murderer, but they could not send him to prison. WHY?

The answer to the puzzle is on this page.

6 *Vocabulary*

Which words would you use to describe these things?

tasty delicious cheap good fresh healthy refreshing juicy

Use the words and the phrases to make advertisements for them.

... in the world.
... you can buy.
... than any other.
... for you and your family.
... in the shops today.
... than anything you have had before.

UNIT 16

What next?

1 Saying what you think

a **How have our lives changed in the last 200, 100 and 50 years?**

Example 100 years ago people washed their clothes by hand, now we use washing machines.
200 years ago most people lived in the country, now they live in cities.

b **How do you think your life will change in the next 10 and 40 years?**

IT IS A COLD, WET NOVEMBER morning in Japan. Yuzo Aichi leaves his flat without a coat or umbrella, gets into the lift and goes to his office. Hiroshi Aichi turns off his computer game and goes to school with his mother. He is wearing only a T-shirt and shorts, Mrs Aichi has a summer dress on.

The Aichi family is not mad. They won't need coats or sweaters. They live on the 480th floor of a 500 storey building. Mr Aichi's office is on the 23rd floor, Hiroshi's school is on the 222nd and the shopping precinct is on the 61st floor. There is even a hospital 50 floors above the shopping precinct. Welcome to Aeropolis, the Japanese city of the future - the whole town inside one 500 storey building.

A large Japanese construction company has planned to build this 2 km high building in the middle of Tokyo Bay. It will take 25 years to build. They say they might begin to build Aeropolis in the next five years. When it is finished it will contain 140,000 residents and 300,000 office workers. The total floor space will be 31 square kilometres. We asked a spokesman for the company if he would like to live up there, in the sky. 'No,' he said. 'I think I'll move into the centre of Tokyo when everyone else moves into Aeropolis. I can't stand heights.'

2 Aeropolis

a **Read the article about a Japanese city in the future and answer the questions.**

1 Where will the city be?
2 How tall will it be?
3 How long will it take to build?
4 When might they start to build it?
5 How much will it cost?

b **In pairs, find the words or phrases in the text which mean:**

1 is wearing a summer dress
2 floor of a building
3 an area where there are shops but no traffic
4 a company which builds houses, offices, etc.
5 people who live in a building
6 a representative who speaks to the public
7 dislike or hate

c **What do you think life will be like in Aeropolis?**

3 Language focus

***will* and *might* for future certainty and possibility**

a **Look at these examples:**

1 They *won't* need coats or sweaters.
2 It *will* contain 140,000 residents.
3 They *might* begin to build Aeropolis in the next five years.

will = something is certain to happen in the future.
might = something is possible in the future but not certain.

What are the negative forms of *will* and *might*?

b **Complete the phrases in column A, using *will*, *won't*, *might* and *might not* and endings from column B.**

A	B
The construction	not finish it before 2020.
The builders	contain a lot of offices.
The building	have a secondary school.
The construction company	be too expensive.
	need millions of yen.
	have 150,000 residents.
	build it in Tokyo Bay.

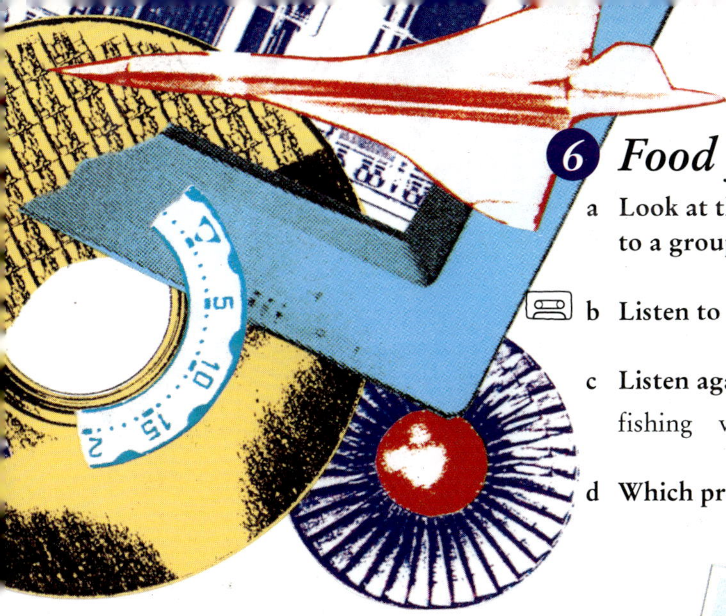

6 *Food for the future*

a Look at the illustrations Professor Davenport is going to use in her talk to a group of students. What do you think she is going to talk about?

b Listen to the talk. Which illustration did she use first, second, third?

c Listen again. What predictions did she make about the following?

fishing   vegetable farms   farming in the desert   robots   solar energy

d Which predictions do you agree with?

4 *Looking to the future*

a Listen to the three conversations about possible changes in the future. How do the speakers feel about a) working from home b) solar energy and c) housework by robots?

b What phrases do they use with *hope* and *think*? What do you notice about the negative responses?

5 *What will happen?*

a In groups, write some predictions for the future 50 or 100 years from now. Write what you think will happen and might happen. Think about:

clothes and fashion   transport
sport   entertainment   money
work   shopping   school   houses
learning languages   machines
holidays

b Tell your predictions to the class. Respond to other students' predictions like this:

I hope . . . / I (don't) think . . .

c Which predictions do the class think are the most certain to happen?

7 *Vocabulary*

Use the words below to complete the sentences in the advertisement.

robot   satellite   answerphone   computer   remote control

UNIT 17

A sense of adventure

1 Saying what you think

a **Look at the holiday photographs. What kind of holidays do they show? Would you like to go on any of these holidays?**

b **In pairs, talk about your holiday likes and dislikes.**

Example What kind of holidays do you like?
Where did you go for your holidays this/last year?
What was it like?

2 Holiday choice

a **Read the articles about holidays and then match them to two of the photographs.**

b **In groups, write down what you think are the positive and negative points about these two holidays. Say if you would like to go to either of these places. Why?/Why not?**

Aigues Tortes, Spain

There are a lot of things you cannot do in the Aigues Tortes National Park – no swimming, no hunting, no camping. In fact, there aren't any cars or caravans in the park at all. However, there are seven special Land Rovers with drivers which take you up the mountains so that you can walk at 2,400 m above sea level.

☆☆☆☆☆☆☆☆☆

There is some magnificant scenery - snow-covered mountains, green valleys, waterfalls and over 50 beautiful clear lakes and plenty of fresh mountain air.

☆☆☆☆☆☆☆☆☆

There aren't any campsites, but there are a few hostels where you can get food and spend the night. There is also some accommodation in the small villages nearby. For further information contact:
Venture Break

The Paradis/Brabant Hotel, Mauritius

This luxurious hotel is situated on 6km of golden beach on the Indian Ocean. There is a private golf course and several other sports facilities, such as water skiing, sailing, windsurfing, scuba diving, deep sea fishing, riding and tennis. There are three restaurants which serve fresh fish and delicious fruits. You can even catch your own fish on a fishing trip with local fishermen.

☆☆☆☆☆☆☆☆☆

With temperatures of 26-28°C and no humidity, the beaches are totally uncrowded and unpolluted, there is very little traffic and the people are amongst the friendliest in the world.

☆☆☆☆☆☆☆☆☆

For further information contact: Flora Duff Torrance, 47 Queen's Reach, East Molesey, Surrey KT8 9DE. Tel 081 979 2462.

3 Language focus

countable and uncountable nouns

Look at these nouns:

Countable	Uncountable
mountain / mountains	scenery / no plural

a **Put these words into the correct column.**

there is / there are

camping cars caravans green valleys crowds snow-covered mountains lakes waterfalls hostels accommodation fresh mountain air traffic facilities fresh fish delicious fruit sports entertainment humidity pollution

b **Now make true sentences about both holidays using the chart below.**

There is	a lot of some not much	There are	a lot of some not many
There isn't	any	There aren't	any

Example *There is some* accommodation in the villages nearby.

Look at the second text and make more sentences using the chart.

A

B

4 *Adventurous ideas*

a **Listen to an interview with a travel agent talking about some unusual holidays and answer the questions.**

1 Which countries does the travel agent mention?

Argentina Belgium Britain Denmark France Germany
India Mexico Sweden Spain Switzerland Zambia

2 In which of these countries does she arrange holidays?

b **Listen again and answer these questions.**

1 What special activities can you do on the three holidays she talks about?

bird watching mountain climbing walking sight seeing
fishing making a raft

2 Would you like to go on any of these holidays? Why?/Why not?

5 *Guesswork*

Think of a country you know. Do not say where it is. In groups, try to guess each person's country by asking questions, like this:

Are there many/a lot of tourists there?
Is it busy/quiet/polluted/clean/expensive?
Can you go there by train from here?

6 *Not good enough*

a **Look at the picture. A guest has just arrived at the hotel. In pairs, discuss what you think she is going to complain about to the manager.**

b **Now listen to the conversation. What does the guest complain about?**

c **Listen again. Notice how the guest complains and the manager apologises. Complete the sentences below.**

1 I would like to __ __ __ .
2 I am __ __ __ the room.
3 __ __ terribly __, madam.
4 __ really __ __ for all this, madam.

d **Can you think of any bad holiday experiences you have had? Tell the class.**

7 *Vocabulary*

a **How many words can you think of for these three types of holiday?**

Example	Beach	City	Country
	sand	sightseeing	walking

b **Look at the parts of holiday advertisements. What kind of holidays do you think they are?**

1 enjoy miles of golden sand, peaceful and uncrowded

2 followed by ten days trekking through the foothills of the Himalayas

3 there is also an optional bus tour, to show you the more unusual sights of the old town

Golden years

1 *Saying what you think*

a Which of these words and phrases describe the different people in the photographs? There may be more than one for each person.

a teenager middle aged very old a toddler
youngish elderly a pensioner in his teens
an infant very young in her thirties

b What do you think are the advantages/disadvantages of being old?

2 *In the family*

a Listen to the three conversations. Match the people talking with the people in the photographs.

b Look at the incomplete sentences. Can you guess what the missing words are? Listen again and see if you were correct.

1 We __ married __ about six months now.
2 His son __ in Australia __ 1980.
3 We __ met since she __ out there.
4 It was very difficult for her, so I __ here with them since __.
5 So many things __ since she __ work.
6 I've lived here __ odd years.
7 I haven't been near a doctor for __.

3 *Language focus*

for and *since*

a Look at these examples:

1 We've been married *for* about six months.
2 I haven't seen her *since* 1962.
3 She hasn't worked *for* a long time.
4 He has been a big help to his mum *since* his dad died.

Can you see the difference between *for* and *since*? Which one refers to a) a point in time in the past b) a period of time?

b Look at the sentences you completed in exercise 2. How many examples with *for* and *since* can you find?

c Put *for* or *since* in front of these time phrases.

six months five years 1988 a few hours
6 o'clock last week ten weeks a long time
years I got married he started work
about five days

Make sentences using similar time phrases.

Example I have lived in Milan *since I* got married.
I haven't played tennis *for* a long time.

4 *Over a century*

a **Read the article and say why Sid Wright is in the news.**

b **Put the events in Sid's life into the correct order.**

1 He had his 103rd birthday.
2 He started to give interviews on the radio.
3 He became a horseman.
4 He retired.
5 His son, Jim, was born.
6 He came to live with Jim and Irene.

c **In groups, decide what you should do if you want to live to 100. Think about:**

diet alcohol tobacco work
climate marriage exercise hobbies

LOCAL PERSONALITY, SID WRIGHT, WAS 103 YESTERDAY.

In the last few months Sid has become well known on local radio. He has given several interviews on farm life at the beginning of the century. Sid left school and became a horseman at the age of 14 and he retired 58 years later. 'I didn't want to retire,' says Sid. 'But the farmer who I worked for sold all his horses. You see, nobody wanted farm horses when the new machinery came in. So when the horses went there was nothing left for me to do.' Yesterday, when people asked him for his recipe for a long life, Sid gave his usual answer. 'No smoking, no drinking, no gambling.' Sid Wright has lived with his son, Jim, and his wife, Irene, for the last 15 years. Both Jim and Irene are in their seventies. Jim has his own ideas about why his father has lived so long. 'My father's never bored. He's interested in everything and everyone. That's what keeps him going.'

5 *A helping hand*

a **Listen to these three conversations with elderly people. Where do you think each conversation takes place?**

b **Listen again. Which phrases do they use to offer, accept and refuse help?**

that's very kind would you like I'm quite all right shall I help
let me I'm fine, really thanks a lot I can manage

6 *Growing old*

In groups, decide:
a) if you would like to live to a very old age. Why/ why not?
b) what things are important to you when you are old. Think about:

your health money
where you live interests
friends transport
family changes in the future

7 *Vocabulary*

a **Where would you see these signs and advertisements?**

b **Do you know the meaning of these words?**

OAP widow widower elderly retirement pension

Fun and games

1 *Saying what you think*

a Do you know all these games? What are they called in your language? Do you know what they're called in English?

b What are popular games in your country?

2 *Playing the game*

a **Read the rules of two games and match them with the pictures.**

A

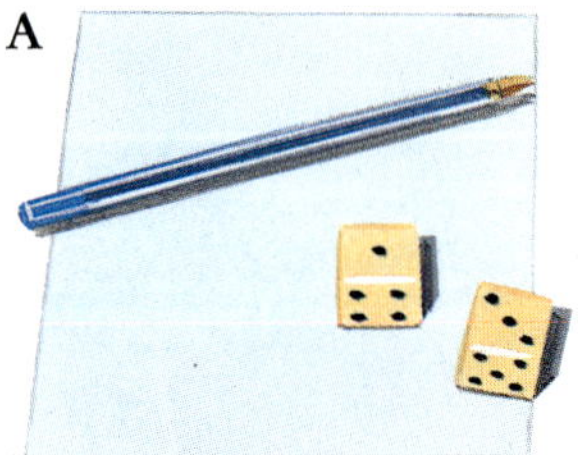

B

b **Are these statements true or false? Correct the false statements.**

1 Only four players can play Chicago.
2 You can play Chicago with two dice or one dice.
3 On the first throw, a 2 gets 2 points.
4 On the last throw, all the players want to get a 12.
5 You have to have an expensive board to play Fan Tan.
6 The players have to put their beans on number 4.
7 The 'banker' has to count the beans into groups of four.
8 At the end of the game, the players have to give the 'banker' five beans.

c **Without looking at the text, explain the rules of Chicago to your partner.**

1

C • H • I • C • A • G • O

For this game you need two dice. You can play with any number of players.

Each player has to throw the dice in turn. If any player gets a 2 (1 on each dice), they score 2 points. When everyone has thrown once, all the players have to throw again. This time they have to score 3 (1 on one dice and 2 on the other). Now all the players throw again and they have to get a 4 (2 on each dice) to score 4 points, and so on, up to 12. The players must not throw more than once for each number. Someone has to write down the scores.

At the end, the winner is the person who scores the most points, so you don't have to get all the numbers correct - you can win with a final score of 12.

C • H • I • C • A • G • O

2

FAN TAN

This is a popular Chinese game. Any number of players can play. You need a board and a bowl of dried beans. You don't have to buy a special board, you can make a simple one.

Each corner of the board has a number; 1, 2, 3 and 4. One of the players is a 'banker' and the 'banker' has to give each player five beans. The players then have to put one of their beans on any number on the corner of the board. The players must not touch these beans.

The 'banker' then takes a handful of beans and puts them in the middle of the board. He/she counts the beans into groups of four. If there are two beans left, the winning number is 2. If there is one bean left, the winning number is 1, and so on.

All the players who put their bean on the winning number can keep the bean and the others have to give theirs to the 'banker'. Continue the game until everyone, except one player, has lost all his/her beans. **This player is the winner.**

3 Language focus

have to, do not have to, must, must not

a **Look at these examples:**

1 Each player *has to* throw the dice.
2 All players *have to* throw again.

Have to **is similar in meaning to** ***must.***

Look at the two texts in exercise 2 and find more examples of have/has to.

b **Look at these examples:**

1 You *don't have to* get all the numbers correct.
2 The players *must not* touch these beans.

The negative of ***have to*** **and the negative of** ***must*** **have different meanings. Which one means a) not necessary b) not allowed?**

Find another example of ***must not*** **and** ***do not have to*** **in the text.**

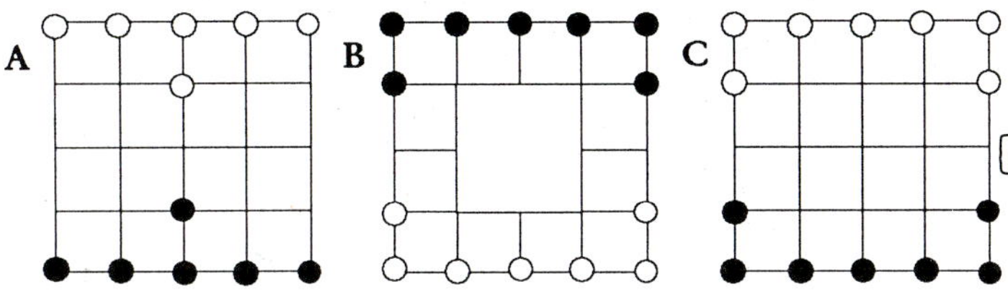

4 Five Field Kono

a **Listen to this conversation where someone describes the rules of Five Field Kono. Which of the three boards is the correct one for the game?**

b **Listen again to the rules of the game. Then use these notes to describe the rules to your partner.**

board / divided into 16 squares / four / four
get a special board / use a piece of paper
player / seven pieces
use special pieces / coins / buttons
put five pieces / bottom / one piece on each side
do the same / top
get your pieces / other side
move diagonally / squares / backwards / forwards
can't go forwards / go backwards

c **Now play the game in pairs. Is it better to move first or not?**

5 Guessing game

In groups, think of a game or sport. Write down two or three rules and tell the class. Can the other students guess what the game or sport is?

Example There are two people. Each person has to hit the other one. You have to wear special gloves. You mustn't hit below the waist. If you fall down, you have to get up before the referee counts to ten.

6 Persuading

a **Listen to this conversation between friends. What expressions do they use to persuade people to play and refuse to play?**

oh, come on   I don't feel like it   just one game
I'm no good at cards   go on   I'm not playing

b **What expressions do they use when they finally agree to play?**

7 Vocabulary

Use the words below to complete the rules of a game.

diagram   remove   rules   example   matchsticks   words

UNIT 20

Animal facts

1 *Saying what you think*

a **Are you afraid of any of these animals? Which one/ ones? Which animals are your favourite or least favourite?**

b **What do you think about a) keeping animals as pets, and b) keeping animals in a zoo or a circus?**

2 *Amazing animals*

a **Read these texts about animals. The last line of each text is missing. Choose the correct line from the sentences 1 to 4. Then match the text with some of the animals in the picture in exercise 1.**

1 It travelled through five states and across the Rocky Mountains in the middle of winter.
2 It does not matter how big the creature.
3 Their bite can kill adult humans.
4 They did not go near.

b **Which of these statements is true? Give examples from the text to show whether statements are true or false.**

1 Piranha fish never attack bigger fish.
2 We do not need to be afraid of spiders. They are not dangerous creatures.
3 The zorilla is a very small animal and it cannot defend itself against larger animals.
4 Many dogs have an excellent sense of direction.

1 The smelliest animal in the world is the African zorilla. If it wants to keep other animals away, it will release a smelly liquid. You can smell the zorilla from 1.5 km. Hunters once saw a zorilla eating a dead zebra and for several hours nine hungry lions watched from a distance.

2 Piranha fish are not very big but they are extremely dangerous. They live in the large rivers of South America. If they smell any injured creature, they will attack.

3 If a dog is lost, it will walk many miles to find its home. Once, in the USA, a Collie dog got lost. His family was 3,200 kms away on holiday. Six months later the dog arrived back home.

4 The most poisonous spiders in the world are the Brazilian wandering spiders. These large, aggressive spiders hide in clothes and shoes. If you leave them alone they won't bother you, but if you disturb them they will bite several times.

c **What is special about the four animals in the texts. Can you think of any other animals with special characteristics?**

3 *Language focus*

first conditional

Look at these examples:

1 *If* they smell any injured creature, they *will* attack.
2 *If* you leave them alone, they *won't* bother you.

In these sentences, if A happens, B will happen.

Example

A	B
Piranha fish smell an injured creature	attack
you leave them alone	not bother you

b **Match the phrases in column A with suitable ones in column B and complete the sentences.**

A	B
you stroke a cat	clean itself
you train a parrot	not come near
a shark smells blood	prepare to attack
a dog gets lost	learn to speak
a crab is in danger	purr
you don't disturb a snake	hide between rocks
a lion smells a zorilla	not bite you
a cockroach touches a human	try to find its way home

4 *Sea zoo*

a Can you find these creatures in the picture?
shark lobster octopus

b Listen to this interview with the manager of a sea zoo and answer the questions.

1 Why do children like the sea zoo?
2 Which sea creatures are the most popular?
3 How does the octopus defend itself?
4 What happens to the female octopus when her eggs hatch?

5 *Working dogs*

a Read this extract from an article about jobs. What do you think the dogs are trained to do?

b What special characteristics do these dogs need? What things do they have to do?

c Can you think of any other 'working' animals?

> these dogs are chosen because of their temperament, stamina and size.
>
> It's important to choose dogs with a calm temperament and they must be strong because they sometimes need to push the owners out of danger. They also need stamina for all the walking they have to do.
>
> We train them from about six weeks old and they learn about traffic, crossing the road, crowds and so on. They must be obedient, good at mixing with all sorts of people and, of course, have good eyesight - they are the owner's second pair of eyes

6 *Strange pets*

a Listen to these two conversations. What strange pets are they talking about?

b Listen again. Which phrases do they use to say they a) don't like and b) are afraid of spiders and snakes?

c In pairs, look at this list of common fears. Put them in order, beginning with the most frightening. Compare the list with another pair.
height flying water dogs cockroaches
going out alone at night spiders snakes
lifts meeting new people

d Which pets are popular? Do you think that all pets should be useful like the working dogs in exercise 5?

7 *Vocabulary*

Match the noise with the animal.

Verb	Noise
miaow	miaow
bark	woof
crow	cock-a-doodle-doo
quack	quack
moo	moo
grunt	oink

What noises do these animals make in your language?

PRACTICE SECTION

1 Match the questions and answers.

1 How are you?
2 What do you do?
3 Are you interested in music?
4 Do you smoke?
5 Are you married?
6 How old are you?
7 Are you French?
8 Do you like sport?

a I'm twenty-one.
b No, I don't.
c Yes. I play alot of tennis.
d I'm fine thanks.
e Yes. I like pop music.
f No, I'm single.
g I'm an engineer.
h No, I'm Spanish.

2 Write the missing words in the sentences.

1 I like Robert. He's very f...................... .
2 This is my sister, Ann.
— P...................... to meet you.
3 Is it important?
— No, it doesn't m...................... .
4 C......................! See you s...................... .
5 He doesn't smoke - he's a n........-...................... .

3 Fill in this form.

Ideal Friends
FRIENDSHIP AGENCY

REGISTRATION FORM
Please use BLOCK LETTERS

Surname ....

First name(s) ....

Mr ☐ Mrs ☐ Miss ☐ Ms ☐ (please tick)

Address ....

....

Phone number ....

Nationality ....

Age 15-20☐ 21-30☐ 31-40☐ 41-50☐ over 50☐

Likes ....

....

Dislikes ....

....

4 Write the questions for these answers.

1 *Is Josephine English?*
— No, she isn't. She's Australian.

2 ....
— I'm not sure. I think she's single.

3 ....
— Friendly? Yes, she's very nice.

4 ....
— I don't know! About twenty-five, I think.

5 ....
— No, she doesn't. She lives in London.

5 Read the text about Carmen and write the verbs in the spaces.

Carmen ....'s.......... *(be)* Spanish and she .... *(be)* nineteen. She .... *(live)* in Barcelona. She .... *(be)* interested in classical music, but she .... *(not like)* pop music. She .... *(not play)* any sport, but she .... *(enjoy)* walking. She .... *(be)* a student and she .... *(want)* an English friend because .... *(want)* to speak English.

1 **Write the questions in this dialogue.**

1 *Where do you live?*
— Near Amsterdam.

2 .... ?
— No, I live in a flat.

3 .... ?
— It's in a modern block. It's very small.

4 .... ?
— No, it hasn't. But it's got a balcony.

5 .... ?
— No, I live by myself.

2 **Answer these questions.**

1 What kind of home do you live in?

....

2 Who do you live with?

....

3 Have you got a garden?

....

4 Have you got a favourite room?

....

3 **a Look at the family tree and complete the sentences.**

1 .... is Edward Jones's mother.
2 Frank Baker is Ella's ....
3 George is .... nephew.
4 .... is William's niece.
5 Ella is Philippa's ....
6 .... is Kate's grandmother.
7 Pat Smith is Edward's ....
8 Kate is Eliza's ....

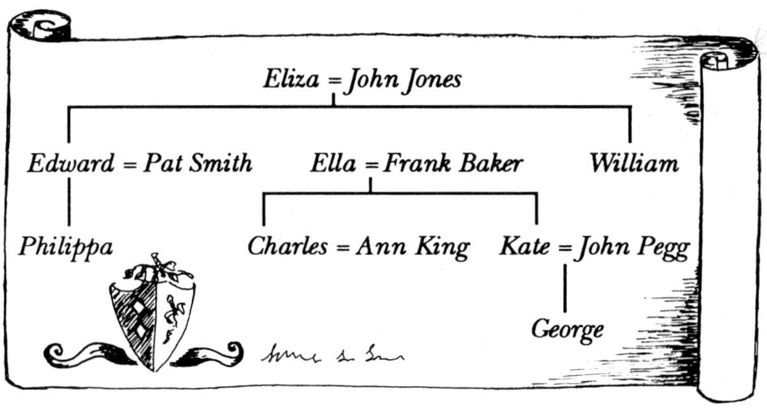

b Use forms of *have got* to make true sentences.

1 Eliza .... two sons, Edward and William.
2 William Jones .... any children.
3 Ella and Frank .... two children, Charles and Kate.
4 Edward and Pat .... a daughter, Philippa.
5 They .... a son.

4 **Put the letters in the right order to make ten words from the unit and complete the lists below.**

1 dwnliiml
2 faso
3 ltbae
4 soheu
5 grus
6 talf
7 debtahsou
8 eadbrwro
9 imrhacra
10 aanrcav

Homes	Furniture
flat	....
....	....
....	....
....	....
....	....

5 **Complete the letter to your penfriend, Mary. Describe your family and your home.**

Dear Mary,
Thank you for your letter. Now I want to write to you about my family and home. I've got ....
....
....
....
I live in .... *It's got* ....
.... , *but it hasn't got* ....
....
I hope you will be able to visit me one day.
love Rosa

1 **Use the prompts to write complete sentences.**

1 Sue/not buy/any new clothes. She/want/save all her money.
Sue isn't buying any new clothes. She wants to save all her money.

2 Paul/want/live in Italy. He/study/Italian.
....

3 Robert/work/very hard. He/not want/fail his exams.
....

4 Lucia/learn/drive. She/want/buy a car next year.
....

5 I/not eat/cakes and sweets. I/want/lose some weight.
....

6 We/not want/cook tonight. We/go/to a restaurant.
....

2 **Put these words in the correct place in the text.**

enjoying takes work saving ambition wants hard to planning easy

James is twenty and he [1] .... to be a doctor. He says, 'I'm studying [2] ...., but I'm [3] .... every minute of it. It [4] .... a long time to become a doctor, and it isn't [5] ...., but if you really want [6] .... study medicine, then hard [7] .... is not a problem. My [8] .... is to work as a doctor in Third World countries and I'm already [9] .... my money and [10] .... my first trip!

3 **Put the words in the sentences in the right order.**

1 eighteen Sara and in lives she Bristol is
Sara is eighteen and she lives in Bristol.

2 photographic she in assistant an is studio a
....

3 is to ambition be her photographer it a
....

4 saving is all money her buy she camera to a new
....

5 wants a photographer to she for national be a newspaper
....

4 **Complete this telephone dialogue between Stephen and the receptionist.**

R: Good morning, Milton Sports Centre.
S: Oh, good morning [1] .... to have some tennis lessons. [2] .... does a lesson cost?
R: Ten pounds for one hour.
S: [3] .... book a lesson for this week?
R: Certainly [4] .... Friday at three o'clock?
S: Friday at three - yes, [5] ....
R: [6] .... your name and address, please?
S: Stephen Bennet, 19 Victoria Street.
R: Thank you Mr Bennet, [7] ....

5 **Look at the advertisements and then answer the questions.**

1

Byland Expeditions

Is your ideal trip an African safari? If so, then this is the expedition for you! Safari expeditions of 2-10 weeks duration, departing from London all year round. This is not a luxury tour, so be prepared for tents and the outdoor life.

2

DREAM ☆ TOURS

Fulfil your life ambitions! Travel to Asia in first class luxury, and discover a wonderful continent. Stay in exotic 5-star hotels in India, Malaysia and Indonesia for 2 to 6 weeks. Departures from London, August to April.

1 How long does the trip to Asia last?
....

2 Do you think the holiday in Asia is expensive?
....

3 Can you go on the Safari in July?
....

4 Can you go on the Asian holiday in December?
....

5 What do you think you need to take with you to Asia?
....

6 What do you think you need to take on Safari?
....

7 Which holiday do you prefer? Why?
....
....

1 **Complete the table of irregular verbs.**

Infinitive	Past simple
see	saw
know	
	became
get	
keep	
	did
go	
	put
	took
	said
leave	

Complete the short biography of the crime novelist, Agatha Christie. Put the verbs in brackets into the past simple.

Agatha Christie was born in 1890 in Torquay, England. Her mother taught her at home until she was sixteen when she .... *(go)* to study singing and the piano in Paris. In 1914, she .... *(marry)* Archibald Christie and they .... *(have)* one daughter. They .... *(divorce)* in 1928. Her second husband .... *(be)* an archaeologist, and together they .... *(travel)* widely. She .... *(start)* writing in 1915. She .... *(create)* the detective Hercules Poirot and she wrote over 70 detective novels. She .... *(die)* in 1976.

3 **Find ten words to do with crime in the wordsquare.**

M	Y	S	T	R	A	N	G	L	E
U	P	V	A	L	N	E	Y	I	D
R	E	B	L	O	C	F	N	K	E
D	M	I	S	A	R	R	E	S	T
E	K	I	L	T	S	O	L	V	E
R	R	L	D	A	Q	P	C	E	C
P	U	N	I	S	H	M	E	N	T
R	K	M	Y	S	T	E	R	Y	I
S	O	N	C	H	A	T	R	E	V
B	E	R	A	P	O	L	I	C	E

4 **Look at the story of the Woman in Black in exercise 4 (page 8 and 67) and answer the questions.**

1 Where was the man arrested?

....

2 What did the papers say about the police?

....

3 Why did the wife shoot off two of her fingers?

....

4 Why didn't the man recognise his wife at first?

....

5 Why did the police release the man?

....

5 **Read these notes about Clive and his Aunt Belinda. Write the story of what you think happened.**

Clive	Aunt Belinda
25 years old	74 years old, but healthy
lived with aunt	had no family except Clive
did not work	thought Clive wasted money
had no money	refused to give him money
was angry with aunt	
liked fruit salad	
knew about poisonous berries	
cooked supper on Fridays	

....

....

....

....

....

....

....

PRACTICE SECTION

1 Write questions for these answers.

1 .... ?
— Three times a week.
2 .... ?
— I usually have a bowl of cereal and a cup of coffee.
3 .... ?
— No, thanks. I don't smoke.
4 .... ?
— No, I usually have a small breakfast.
5 .... ?
— About 55 kilos.

2 Use these words and phrases to complete the sentences.

diet energy weigh vegetarian lose weight
put on weight exercise fattening

1 People on health farms often ....
2 I have to be careful what I eat because I .... very easily.
3 He good at sport - he's got a lot of ....
4 You need to .... to keep fit.
5 How often do you .... yourself?
6 Some people, like athletes, have a special ....
7 She doesn't eat meat. She's a ....
8 I like chocolate, but it's very ....

3 Put the letters in the right order to make ten words about food from the unit.

1 trufi	4 hotrygu	7 sannaab
2 lchtaoeco	5 spcih	8 klim
3 tacror	6 tbture	

4 Put the words in the sentences in the right order.

1 always healthy don't people meals eat
People ....
2 chocolate rarely I eat
....
3 how exercise do often take you?
....
4 enough dancers eat sometimes don't food
....
5 never goes swimming she
....
6 I every go usually a year to farm health
....

5 Use the prompts to write short dialogues.

1 like/a drink? (accept)
Would you like a drink?
—Yes, please.
2 Like/tea or coffee? (refuse both)
....
....
3 got/any orange juice? (yes)
....
....
4 How/an ice-cream? (refuse)
....
....
5 want/some cake? (accept)
....
....

6 Read the article from the magazine. Then write a short paragraph about what you eat on a typical day.

DIET

We asked doctors and health experts to examine the diets off our women with very different lives. The results were extremely interesting!

This is what Sonia, an executive in an international company, eats on a typical day.

'I'm usually too busy for breakfast, so I just have a cup of coffee, or sometimes a piece of toast before I leave for the office. I always keep a packet of biscuits in my drawer at work and I have one with my coffee at about eleven o'clock. Sometimes I have a bar of chocolate, but usually I wait until lunchtime when I have a bowl of soup, or perhaps a salad and an orange juice. I have a cup of tea about three o'clock, if I'm not in a meeting (which I usually am!). I cook dinner when I get home - fish or chicken and vegetables - something like that. Sometimes I have a bowl of ice-cream too, but usually I just have some fruit. When I work late, which often happens, I buy a take-away Chinese meal or a pizza on the way home!

....
....
....
....
....
....
....
....

1 Put these words in the correct place in the text.

factory produces with unusual had
play wanted balls works never

Twenty-eight-year-old Elaine Nickerson has a very [1] unusual job. She [2] works in a tennis ball [3] factory in the north of England. The factory [4] produces several million balls every year - and 34,000 of those [5] balls are for the Wimbledon tennis fortnight in June! Elaine tests each ball and cuts off any extra pieces of material [6] with a small pair of scissors. But she says, 'I've [7] never been to Wimbledon, and I can't [8] play tennis!' The factory once [9] had tennis courts, but nobody [10] wanted to play tennis.

2 Look at these prompts and write questions about Elaine Nickerson and her job.

1 What/factory make?

....

2 How old/Elaine?

....

3 How many/balls/factory produce?

....

4 What/Elaine do?

....

5 Elaine/play tennis?

....

3 Now write the answers to the questions in exercise 2.

1 ....
2 ....
3 ....
4 ....
5 ....

4 Complete the sentences using *too* and *very*.

1 I'd like to be a model but I'm .... short.
2 Factory work is sometimes .... boring.
3 Some people work .... hard and then they are .... tired to go out in the evening.
4 Teaching is a .... enjoyable job.
5 Many people think that the army is .... hard for women.

5 a What do you like doing in your free time? Write three answers.

I like ....
I enjoy ....
I love ....

b Write three things you don't like doing.

I don't like ...., ... *or* ....

6 Read the clues and complete the crossword. All the answers are words from Unit 6.

Across
1 Not inside. In the open air.
2 For a lot of jobs you need qualifications, but you also need ....
3 He plays music in the street.
4 Andrew e...................... working as a model.
5 'Position' m...................... the same as 'job'.

Down
6 It's a t...................... job - it's only for six weeks.
7 You must have this to drive a car.
8 Very, very important.

1 **Ted is in hospital with a broken leg. What can he do? What can't he do? Use these words to make sentences about Ted.**

newspapers and magazines   television   tennis
visitors   bath   radio   the garden   his toes

1 *He can read newspapers and magazines.*
2 ....
3 ....
4 ....
5 ....
6 ....
7 ....
8 ....

2 a **Read this advertisement carefully.**

HELP! Mother's help needed for the summer holiday. Our mother's help likes children under eight, drives, swims, tells stories, paints, cooks meals, is patient, very fit and over eighteen. If you are this person, **telephone 83283 and ask for Mrs Williams.**

Are these sentences True or False?

1 Mrs Williams' children are eight years old.
2 The job is for one year.
3 She doesn't want a sixteen-year-old.
4 She wants someone who can drive.

b **You are talking to Mrs Williams on the telephone. She is asking you a lot of questions. Complete her questions.**

1 .... old .... you?
2 .... drive?
3 .... like children?
4 .... meals?
5 .... swim?

c **Now write your answers to Mrs Williams' questions.**

1 ....
2 ....
3 ....
4 ....
5 ....

3 **Put these words into the correct place in the text.**

couldn't   thought   had   spoke   can't   are
was   communicate   didn't answer
doesn't matter

When I was at school some people [1] .... I was stupid. The problem was that I [2] .... deaf. People [3] .... to me, but I [4] .... hear them, so I [5] .... them. Fortunately, I [6] .... a very nice teacher. Things [7] .... different now. Nowadays people try to think about what you can do, not what you [8] .... do. I can [9] .... with sign language and I have an interesting job. I'm a computer operator and for that job it really [10] .... if you can't hear.

4 a **You are on holiday with a friend. You can't find your hotel. Look at the dialogue and underline two suggestions.**

Y: Look, we're lost. Why don't we ask someone?
F: I don't like asking people.
Y: Well, let's buy a map then.
F: That's a good idea.

b **Now make suggestions for these situations.**

1 You are sightseeing. You are very tired and you can't walk any more.
2 You are hungry and thirsty.
3 It's too hot to go sightseeing. You want to relax and keep cool.

5 **Find eight words to do with language and communication in the wordsquare.**

O	L	M	P	E	A	K	C	V	I
T	R	A	N	S	L	A	T	E	F
L	S	A	N	T	W	R	I	T	E
N	E	S	I	G	N	I	B	D	G
E	J	Y	V	O	U	C	K	Q	S
D	A	M	T	W	R	A	I	S	C
S	O	B	O	R	V	I	G	P	N
T	C	O	D	E	H	I	N	E	T
E	H	L	S	A	E	O	R	A	O
A	T	I	N	D	O	T	I	K	B

PRACTICE SECTION

1 Look at the text about Houdini on page 15, Unit 8. Then look at these sentences. They are all wrong. Can you correct them?

1 Harry Houdini died in 1920.
No, he didn't. He died in 1926.
2 His real name was Ehrich Houdin.
No, it wasn't..
3 He was born in Bulgaria.
....
4 He went to America when he was twenty-one.
....
5 He became famous when he joined a circus.
....
6 He began to do magic tricks in the 1920s.
....
7 Once, some people put him in a box and threw him into the sea.
....
8 He died from his dangerous tricks.
....

2 Read the notes about Charles Lindbergh.

Born: 1902, Detroit, USA.
Became famous: 1927. Flew first non-stop solo flight across Atlantic, New York - Paris.
Career: left university in second year to join flying school; did flying shows; later was airmail pilot; 1926 businessmen helped with money to try Atlantic flight; plane called 'Spirit of St Louis'; flight took 33 hours.
Died: 1974, Hawaii, USA.

Now complete the questions for these answers.

1 Where .... ?
— In Detroit.
2 When .... ?
— In 1974.
3 Why .... famous?
— He was the first man to fly solo across the Atlantic.
4 .... university?
— No, he didn't.
5 What .... ?
— The 'Spirit of St Louis'.
6 How long .... ?
— It took 33 hours.

3 Put the verbs in brackets into the past simple.

The Roaring Twenties .... *(be)* the name given to the 1920s in the USA. Americans .... *(want)* to enjoy themselves after the First World War. People .... *(make)* lots of money and fashions .... *(change)*. They .... *(begin)* to buy cars and TVs and .... *(go)* out to jazz clubs and bars. Women .... *(wear)* short skirts and .... *(cut)* their hair. Many people .... *(be)* very rich during the twenties - until the Wall Street Crash in 1929, when they .... *(lose)* a lot of money.

4 Match the words in A with their meaning in B.

A	B
1 famous	a go to live in another country
2 escape	b a room you put a prisoner in
3 emigrate	c not safe
4 teens	d ten years
5 tramp	e well-known
6 cell	f get out/get away
7 decade	g the years from 13-19
8 dangerous	h someone with no home, no job, no money

5 a Put the letters in the right order to make four words connected with Houdini's life.

1 srucci
2 gciamnia
3 niahc
4 csrtik

b Now find four words about money and business.

1 lcfniniaa
2 mkarte
3 mayocpn
4 lolasrd

PRACTICE SECTION

1 **Read the text and underline words or phrases which mean the same as:**

1 use carelessly
2 wash down with lots of water
3 the ordinary British person
4 used again
5 the pipe to carry dirty water away from your house

Saving Water

In Britain people waste a lot of water. Let's think about drinking quality water. We flush about 30% of it down the toilet, we wash ourselves in 17%, and we put another 12% through washing machines and dishwashers. The average Briton uses 45,000 litres of water every year. That's a lot of water! In industry people are trying to save water. Some water is recycled ten times before it goes down the drain.

2 **Look at the pictures and write sentences saying what you can do to help the environment.**

1 *Don't have a bath. Have a shower instead.*
2 ....
3 ....
4 ....
5 ....

3 **Give your opinion about the statements below. Use *I agree/I don't agree, I think, I feel.***

1 Red meat is bad for you.
I don't agree. I think it's an important part of our diet.
2 We have too many cars on our roads.
....
3 Pollution is the biggest problem in the world today.
....
4 It's wrong to kill animals to make fur coats.
....
5 It's all right to smoke in public places.
....

4 **Look at the map and read the directions to the recycling factory.**

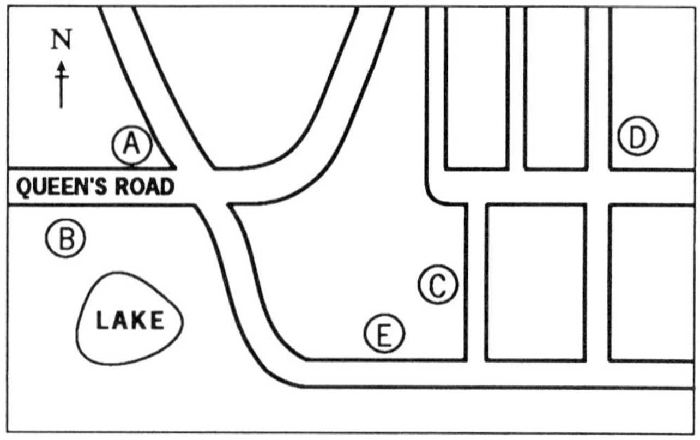

Come into the town from the west, using Queen's Road. There is a wood on your right. After the wood, you'll see a lake and then a petrol station on the corner on your left. Turn right at the crossroads and follow the road until you reach the bottle bank on your left. Turn left a few metres after the bottle bank and follow the road past the shops on your left. Opposite the shops are four litter bins. At the end of the road turn right, then take the second turning on the left. The recycling factory is just after the school on your right.

1 What can you find at A, B, C, D and E?
2 Mark the four litter bins and the recycling factory in the correct places on the map.
3 You are at the recycling factory and someone asks you the way to the petrol station. Write the directions .

....
....
....
....

5 **Find eight words to do with pollution and the environment in the wordsquare.**

I	T	B	O	S	F	D	P	H	D
C	B	L	I	T	T	E	R	T	I
T	K	N	V	W	S	O	U	T	S
R	C	G	N	A	D	J	B	R	P
A	E	R	O	S	O	L	B	E	O
F	C	N	L	T	L	O	I	V	S
F	S	L	E	E	W	H	S	T	A
I	R	A	S	R	D	Q	H	F	B
C	A	O	V	A	G	O	U	B	L
H	K	T	R	E	C	Y	C	L	E

1 **Read the letter and complete the table. Decide if the present continuous is used to talk about the present or the future.**

Dear Gill

Thank you for the brochure about Loch Fyne Hotel - it looks wonderful. I'm coming to Scotland in June, so please book a room for us for two weeks in June. I'm stopping in Edinburgh on the way and I'm staying with some friends there for a couple of days.

I'm writing a new book at the moment, so I'm working very hard. I'm travelling to London on Thursday on business, but in the evening I'm meeting my sister and we're going to the theatre.

I'm looking forward to my trip to Scotland!

See you soon

Love

Sarah

present continuous for the present	present continuous for the future
I'm writing	*I'm coming*

2 **Write complete sentences using the prompts.**

1 What/do/this weekend?
What are you doing this weekend?

2 I/go/to the cinema tomorrow.

....

3 Where/you/stay/on holiday?

....

4 We/hire/fancy dress costumes for the party.

....

5 She/play/tennis on Monday.

....

6 You/see/your aunt this weekend?

....

7 What/you/do tomorrow?

....

8 I/have/some friends to dinner.

....

3 **What are your plans for the weekend? Complete this short paragraph using the present continuous (*I'm ...ing*).**

On Saturday morning ....

....

....

.... *In the evening*

....

....

On Sunday ....

....

National Opera House: Festival Opera Company presents **TURANDOT**. 5 nights only, July 1-5 at 7.30 p.m. Tickets available in advance from Box Office at £15, £20, £30. **Tel: 3185203**

4 **Read the advertisement and complete the two dialogues between Jenny, Peter and the receptionist.**

a P: Oh look. *Turandot* is on at the National Opera House 1 .... like to go?
J: Yes, 2 .... I really like opera, you know.
P: When would 3 .... ? How 4 .... Tuesday evening?
J: Oh 5 .... I'm afraid 6 ....
P: 7 .... we go on Wednesday, then?
J: Yes. 8 ....
P: Right. I'll phone the box office and book the tickets.

b R: Good morning. 1 .... help you?
P: Yes. 2 .... to book some tickets for Wednesday evening.
R: Certainly. How many 3 .... ?
P: Two, 4 ....
R: Would 5 .... £15, £20 or £25 tickets?
P: I think 6 .... , please.
R: So that's two £15 tickets for Wednesday evening.
P: 7 .... right 8 .... very much.

5 **Put the letters in the right order to make eight activities for leisure time.**

1 flog
2 sigifhn
3 oteptyr
4 rcuaphniatg
5 madra
6 isfigwdurnn
7 knawlig
8 gntiapin

1 Put these words in the correct place to complete the text.

bought own borrow rented decided give up plans asked refused project persuaded lend

Fifteen-year-old Simon Kemp [1] .... that he wanted a farm at the age of thirteen. He worked on a school farm [2] .... and then [3] .... his parents if he could have his [4] .... animals. At first they [5] .... , but Simon didn't [6] .... Finally he [7] .... them that he was serious about the idea and they agreed to [8] .... him the money to buy six hens. He [9] .... a field and soon he [10] .... two cows and some sheep as well. He knows what his [11] .... are for the future. 'I'm going into farming, and I'll [12] .... the money I need to do it from the bank.'

2 Look at exercise 4 on page 22 and complete the questions using *how much* and *how many*.

1 .... partners has Mandy got?
2 .... did they need to buy the machinery?
3 .... banks did they ask to lend them money?
4 .... companies lent them money?
5 .... did they need to borrow from the bank?
6 .... orders have they got at the moment?

3 Now answer the questions in exercise 2.

1 ....
2 ....
3 ....
4 ....
5 ....
6 ....

4 Match the words in A with their meanings in B.

A	B
1 prize	a not a profit
2 borrow	b this is where you keep the money in a shop
3 refuse	c money that you have borrowed
4 cash	d something you win in a competition
5 till	e an opportunity
6 loss	f a group of people working together
7 chance	g the opposite of 'give'
8 loan	h the opposite of 'lend'
9 team	i banknotes and coins - not a cheque
10 receive	j the opposite of 'accept'

5 What do you say when somebody says:

1 I've just won £5,000 in a competition!
That's fantastic!
2 My cat died last week.
....
3 I went for an interview, but I didn't get the job.
....
4 My parents are buying me a car for my eighteenth birthday.
....
5 I'm afraid I can't come to the party - I'm working late tomorrow.
....
6 We're getting married in June.
....
7 I got 90% in my college exam.
....
8 Business is very bad at the moment.
....

UNIT 12

PRACTICE SECTION

1 Read the text and answer the questions.

I got married twenty-five years ago. I was very young, just seventeen, and he was twenty-five. I was really in love, and had very romantic ideas about marriage. I thought we would live happily ever after. Well, it hasn't all been like that. We had three children very quickly so there was never any spare money, and I seemed to spend all my time washing, cleaning and talking baby talk! My husband never understood - he thought I had an easy life!

However, now the children are grown up, I can go out more, and I work part-time too. My husband and I are getting to know each other again - and the children are going to organise a party for us, to celebrate our silver wedding anniversary! I'm looking forward to the next twenty-five years.

1 How old is the woman now?

....

2 What did she think about marriage when she was seventeen?

....

3 Why did her husband think she had an easy life?

....

4 What does she do now?

....

5 What is going to happen for their silver wedding?

....

6 Who is going to organise the party?

....

2 Write questions from the prompts using *going to* + infinitive.

1 When/she/start work?
When is she going to start work?

2 Where/you/live?

....

3 Who/look after/the children?

....

4 You/get married/this year?

....

5 When/they/have the party?

....

6 Who/come/to the wedding?

....

3 Answer these questions about your future plans.

1 What are you going to do this evening?

....

2 Who are you going to see tomorrow?

....

3 What are you going to do next week?

....

4 What are you going to do this Christmas?

....

4 Write a short paragraph about your holiday plans using these notes.

spend next holiday (place)
get there (plane, train, etc.)
stay (hotel, tent, etc.)
see/do (sightsee, sunbathe, etc.)

....

....

....

....

....

....

....

....

....

....

5 Put these words in the correct place to complete the conversation between Jane, Liz and Maria.

remember so married disagree waste agree right special

J: I think people spend too much money on weddings. It's a [1] .... of money.
L: Mmm. I think [2] .... too.
M: Oh. I don't [3] .... I mean - it's a very [4] .... day - once in a lifetime.
J: But when you're young and you're going to get [5] .... you need to save all your money for your house and furniture.
L: Yes, that's [6] ....
M: Well, I [7] .... Your wedding day is a day to [8] .... with all your friends and family there.

PRACTICE SECTION

1 Your friend is going on holiday to China. Tell him/her the things that he/she *must* or *should* do, using the prompts.

1 (travellers cheques)
You should get some travellers cheques from the bank.
2 (passport)
....
3 (guide book)
....
4 (light clothes)
....
5 (visa)
....
6 (camera)
....

2 Match the sentences in A with the responses in B.

A	B
1 It's going to rain today.	a You should buy a tent.
2 I'm going to Russia soon.	b You must sign the entry form.
3 I'm going on a camping holiday.	c You should take an umbrella.
4 The front door is locked.	d Can you open the window?
5 I'm going to the south of Spain.	e You should take some sun cream with you.
6 I'm going to enter this holiday competition.	f You must get a visa.
7 It's too hot in here.	g Don't worry. You can get in the side door.

3 a Put these words in the correct place to complete the text.

usually should country mild city speak
trip currency weather looks

Malta is a small [1] .... It is an island in the Mediterranean, between Italy and Libya. Maltese people [2] .... Maltese, English or Italian. The [3] .... is the Maltese pound and the capital [4] .... is Valetta.

The summers are [5] .... very hot and the winters [6] .... The best time to go is in the spring, when the countryside [7] .... wonderful, before the [8] .... gets too hot. Visitors [9] .... spend some time in Valetta, which is a very old and interesting city. They should also take a [10] .... by boat to the beautiful island of Gozo.

b Now write about your country. Describe its position, languages, currency, capital city and weather. Give some advice about when to go and what to see.

....
....
....
....
....
....

4 Read the extracts from an expedition handbook and answer the questions.

Success depends on good planning and careful preparation.

The best way to keep warm is with several layers of clothing. ***Two thin pullovers are better than one thick one.***

Shoes and trainers are not suitable. They do not support or protect your ankles enough on rough ground. ***You should buy proper walking boots.***

Do not forget you are carrying everything with you -clothes, tent, stoves, fuel, food - enough to survive for 72 hours in possibly bad conditions. ***You must eat well.***

1 What kind of expedition do you think it is?
....
2 What is the best way to keep warm?
....
3 What should you wear on your feet?
....
4 What might the weather be like?
....
5 Why must you eat well?
....
6 Why are you carrying everything with you?
....

5 Underline the 'odd man out' in each group.

1 September May October <u>winter</u>
2 lire coins pounds marks
3 travel visa passport boarding card
4 sweater jacket seatbelt trousers
5 cash bill cheque credit card
6 mild warm rainy weather

1 Complete the dialogue between Angela and the reporter using the verbs in brackets. Use the present perfect.

R: How long .... you .... *(be)* a world class athlete?
A: For about ten years now.
R: .... you always .... *(be)* so serious about training?
A: Oh, yes, because I .... always .... *(want)* to be the best.
R: .... you .... *(make)* a lot of money in the last ten years?
A: Well, I .... already .... *(earn)* £25,000 this year - and it's only July!

2 Complete the sentences with these verbs, using the past simple or the present perfect.

write score go study become

1 He .... mathematics since the age of twelve.
2 She .... her first novel when she was fifteen.
3 I .... famous about five years ago.
4 I'm terrible at football - I .... never .... a goal in my life!
5 Evelyn .... to many different countries with orchestras.

3 a Look at these notes and answer the questions.

Jan Tyler
TV reporter - reported news from every continent - been to 43 different countries
33 - red hair, green eyes - unmarried
French at university - worked in local radio - local TV - national TV (5 years now)

1 What does Jan Tyler do?
2 How old is she?
3 Is she married or single?
4 How many countries has she been to?
5 What did she study at university?
6 What other jobs has she done?

b Now write a paragraph about Jan Tyler, using the notes to help you.

Jan Tyler is a TV reporter. She ....
....
....
....
....

4 Complete the reporter's interview with a cyclist.

R: [1] .... just been?
C: I've been on a trip along the Nile - from Cairo to Khartoum by bike!
R: How long [2] .... ?
C: It took about six months.
R: [3] .... this kind of trip before?
C: Yes. Last year I went to the Himalayas with my bike.
R: [4] .... !
C: Well, it's true.
R: Have you [5] .... ?
C: Yes, and I'm going to publish it next summer.

5 Answer the clues to complete the crossword.

Across
1 A special ability.
2 A female hero.
3 A book which you write about your life.
4 A person who never goes out or sees people at all.

Down
5 Muhammed Ali was World .... in boxing.
6 Another word for a 'film'.
7 Deaf people often learn to .... -read.
8 A very, very clever person.
9 Very surprised, or amazed.

PRACTICE SECTION

1 **Complete the table with the comparative and superlative form of each adjective.**

Adjective	Comparative	Superlative
old	*older*	*oldest*
big		
noisy		
famous		
aggressive		
quiet		
busy		
delicious		
good		
bossy		

2 a **Read the text and look at the picture of the Smith children below. Then write down the name and age of each person in the picture.**

1 ....
2 ....
3 ....
4 ....
5 ....
6 ....

The oldest child in the Smith family is Ted. He's 16. Pat, Penny and Poppy are triplets and they are two years younger than Ted. Penny's the tallest of the triplets and Poppy is the one with the biggest smile. The twins, Bill and Ben, were born five years after the triplets. Ben has his hair longer than Bill, so people know who he is. He's twenty minutes older than Bill and he's very proud of that.

b **Are these statements true or false? Correct the false statements.**

1 The twins are older than the triplets.
2 Bill and Ben are six years older than Ted.
3 Penny's taller than Poppy.
4 Ben's the youngest of the Smiths.
5 Poppy looks the happiest.

3 **Put these words in the correct place to complete the text.**

own best called individual become
tastes both differences could other

I think that all twins have a close relationship. My sister, Betty, and I are identical in most ways and have very similar [1] .... , but there are little [2] .... At school we never really had our [3] .... personalities - everybody just [4] .... us 'the twins'. Sometimes I pretended to be Betty, just to see if anybody could tell the difference. We went to different universities, which was a good thing, because our friends there knew us as [5] .... people, not one of a pair. We've [6] .... closer as we've got older, and we 1 [7] .... live in the same town again. We see each [8] .... every day and Betty is definitely the [9] .... friend I have got!

4 **Write a short paragraph describing the similarities and differences between you and your brother/sister or your best friend.**

....
....
....
....
....
....
....
....

5 **Put the letters in the right order to make adjectives which describe personality.**

1 odmyo
2 synio
3 trigbh
4 ellivy
5 griagesevs
6 sboys
7 uitqe

1 a Read the two newspaper articles. Then match the words in list A with their meanings in list B.

A LOOK INTO THE FUTURE

Seven years later than planned, the Hubble Space Telescope went into space yesterday. It was taken up by space shuttle Discovery from Cape Canaveral. Hundreds of excited astronomers watched as it left.
The telescope will use the biggest map of the night sky ever made. The map records 19 million objects in space and is written on 400 computer disks.
Hubble will look for signs of intelligent alien life. It will also try to discover how much longer intelligent life in the universe can be expected to continue. An important

ARTICLE 1 (25 APRIL 1990)

AN EXPENSIVE MISTAKE?

All is not well with the Hubble Space Telescope. The quality of images coming back to Earth are poorer than expected. Astronomers think that one of the telescope's mirrors might be the wrong shape. NASA has started an investigation.

ARTICLE 2 (2 JULY 1990)

A	B
1 telescope	a from another world
2 space shuttle	b form (for example, 'square' or 'round')
3 astronomers	c something you use to look at the stars
4 alien	d pictures
5 images	e people who study the stars and planets
6 shape	f a type of space ship

b Now read the articles again and write the answers to these questions.

Article 1

1 What is the full name of the telescope?

....

2 How did it get into space?

....

3 How did the astronomers feel when it left?

....

4 What will the telescope do?

....

Article 2

1 Why do astronomers think there is something wrong?

....

2 What might be wrong?

....

2 Complete these sentences using *will, won't* or *might*.

1 I haven't decided. I .... go to Spain or I .... go to Greece for my holiday.
2 I've got so much work to do, I .... get it finished tonight.
3 It .... be very hot in Tunisia in August.
4 The sun is shining now but it .... rain later.
5 No, I've decided. I .... go to the party tonight - I'm too tired.
6 I'm not sure about going to the cinema. I .... not like the film.

3 Make predictions about life in 50 years' time, using the prompts.

1 (robots)
Most people will have robots in their homes.
2 (500 storey buildings)
....
3 (solar energy)
....
4 (pollution)
....
5 (enough to eat)
....
6 (grow food in space)
....
7 (work from home)
....

4 Respond to these predictions using *I hope so, I hope not, I think so* and I *don't think so.*

5 Complete the sentences with the right word.

1 There's a shopping p...................... in the centre of town.
2 There are no workers in the factory. The cars are made by r...................... .
3 An a...................... alarm rings if anybody enters the room.
4 I can't s...................... answerphones because I find it difficult to speak to a machine.

5 I used the r...................... control to turn off the TV.
6 We want John to be the s...................... for our group because he explains things so well.

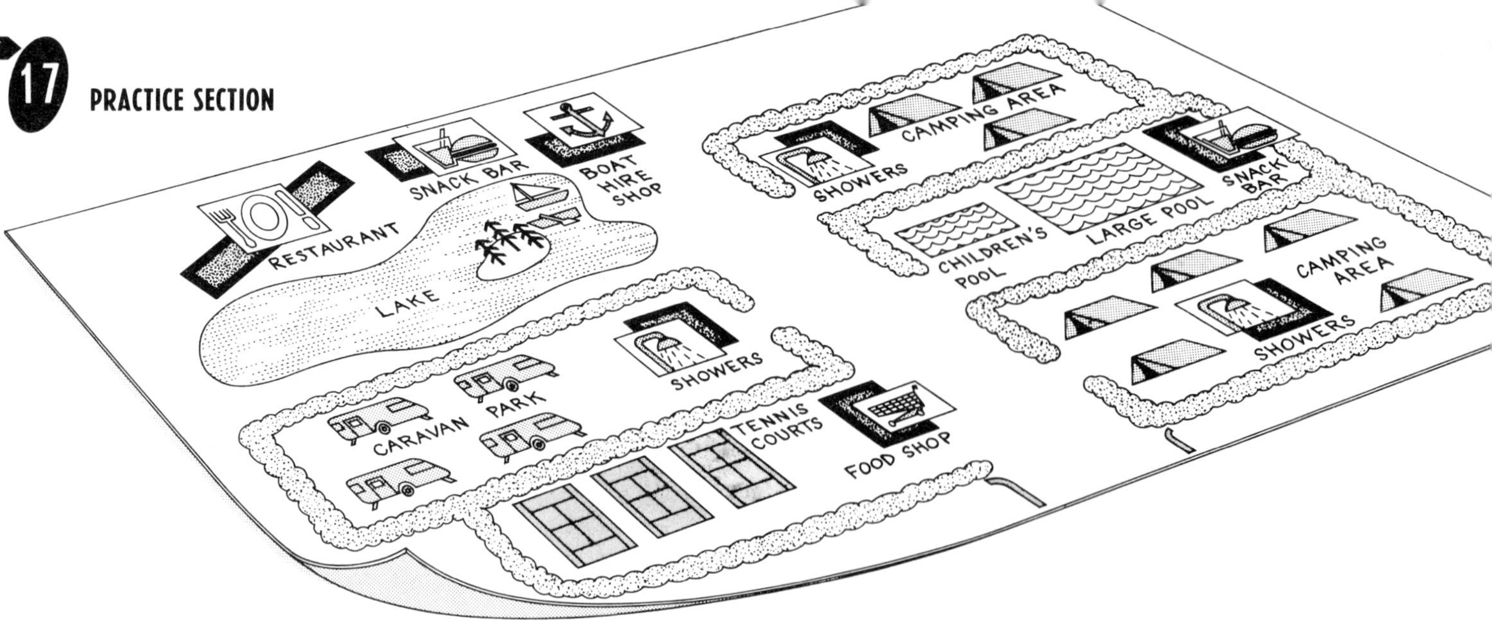

1 **Look at the map of the campsite and complete the sentences.**

1 (swimming pool) *There are two swimming pools.*
2 (restaurant) ....
3 (showers) ....
4 (lake) ....
5 (tennis court) ....
6 (food shop) ....
7 (boat hirc shop) ....
8 (snack bar) ....

2 **Read the text and then decide if the statements are True or False. Correct the false statements.**

WHERE TO STAY ➤➤➤➤

Wherever you go in France, there are plenty of places to stay. Campsites are usually excellent and cheap, and the luxury hotels are some of the best in the world. Between these two is a variety of small hotels and pensions with very reasonable prices. If you like to do it yourself, there is a lot to choose from: tents, chalets, villas, farm cottages. Gites de France are holiday homes in the country which are now very popular.

For more information contact:
French Tourist Office, 178 Piccadilly, London W1V OAL

1 There are a lot of places to stay in France.
2 Campsites are always very good.
3 Pensions are expensive places to stay.
4 A *gite* is a country holiday home.
5 A lot of people like staying in gites.
6 To find out more you must write to Paris.

3 **Complete the text using these words.**

mountains friendly scenery facilities valley centre is there

Mayrhofen is in the Austrian Tyrol. The nearby [1] .... are over 3,300 m high and the [2] .... is magnificent. [3] .... are also chairlifts to take you up the mountains and a railway that goes through the [4] .... Mayrhofen is a [5] .... Tyrolean village with little traffic and plenty of [6] .... - swimming pools, horse riding, tennis and shops. In the evening there [7] .... entertainment at the local cafés and bars.

4 **Now read the text about Mayrhofen again and then write a similar description of your home town or a holiday resort you know.**

....
....
....
....
....
....

5 **Correct this text. There are five grammar mistakes and five spelling mistakes.**

There is many countries where you can go on a sports holiday. Outdoor activitys are very popular and many peopel are wanting to learn a new sport. Try flying and see some wonderful sceneries, or go rafting or learn tenis. Have you any ideas about what you would like to doing? If so write to the tourist ofice of the country you want to visit and they will send you any brochures.

1 Complete the sentences using the present perfect for the verbs in brackets, and *for* or *since*.

1 He .... *(be)* a mechanic .... ten years.
2 She .... *(know)* Mary .... they were at school.
3 He .... *(have)* that car .... 1980.
4 They .... *(be married)* .... last July.
5 We .... *(not see)* Robert .... ages.
6 She .... *(not write)* to me .... over a year.

2 Read the text and then write sentences about Janet Spender, using the prompts in brackets.

Janet Spender is 70 years old. She was born in London but moved to Cobden, a small village in the country, 40 years ago. She worked as a teacher and then retired when she was 60. Her husband died six years ago, so she lives alone, with Sooty, her cat. She bought Sooty the year after her husband died, for company. But she isn't lonely because she has a lot of friends in Cobden. Her newest and youngest friend is Susie. Susie is just five years old and her family moved in next door last year. Susie loves talking to Janet and comes to see her every day.

1 (live in Cobden)
Janet has lived in Cobden for 40 years.
2 (be retired) ....
3 (live alone) ....
4 (have a cat) ....
5 (live next door) ....

3 a Write a short paragraph about a person you know well like the paragraph in exercise 2.

....
....
....
....

b Now write 4 sentences about the person.

.... for ....
.... for ....
.... since ....
.... since ....

4 Write the dialogue between a young man and an old lady. Try to use these words.

kind let shall trouble manage

Robert	Mrs Pevensey
Greet Mrs Pevensey. Offer to carry suitcase.	Thank Robert.
Offer to call a taxi.	Refuse - you want to take the bus.
Offer to give Mrs Pevensey a lift in your car.	Thank Robert. Ask if he is sure.
Say yes, you've got plenty of time.	Thank Robert and accept.

5 Answer the clues to complete the crossword.

Across
1 Another word for 'old'.
2 A holiday you go on when you get married.
3 A man whose wife has died.
4 'Shall I help you?' 'No, thanks. I can .... '.

Down

5 Money you get after you retire.
6 I haven't cleaned the top window box because I can't .... it.
7 The son of your daughter.
8 A young child who has just learnt to walk.

PRACTICE SECTION

1 **Complete these sentences with *have to, don't have to* or *mustn't*.**

In Chess:

- you [1] .... learn how each piece moves.
- you [2] .... let your opponent take your king.
- you [3] .... think carefully before you move.
- you [4] .... finish the game within a certain time.

In Scrabble:

- you [5] .... make words across and/or down.
- you [6] .... use all your letters at the same time.
- you [7] .... look at other people's letters.
- you [8] .... spell words correctly.

2 **a Complete the text using these words.**

owner   over   dictionary   invented   couldn't
scores   since   tried   games   had

Scrabble was originally [1] .... by a man called Alfred Butts, in New York. In 1948 a friend of his [2] .... marketing it commercially, but it didn't sell very well. Then, in 1952, the [3] .... of a large department store in New York played the game while he was on holiday. When he came back tried to buy it in his own store, but [4] .... He told his managers that they [5] .... to stock it. Soon other stores started to do the same, and [6] .... then it has become one of the most popular [7] .... of the century. I play it two or three times a week and almost always score [8] .... 400. I once got SQUEEZE as the first word! I think you have to know your [9] .... inside out and understand the strategies of the game if you want to get high [10] .... , but you can enjoy yourself at any level.

b Now answer these questions about the text.

1 Who invented Scrabble?

....

2 Why did the department store owner try to buy the game?

....

3 Why did Scrabble start to sell more successfully?

....

4 Why do you think the writer was pleased with the word SQUEEZE?

....

3 **Write a few sentences to explain the rules of a game or sport you know well.**

....

....

....

....

....

....

....

....

4 **Harry is trying to persuade his friend Felix to play golf. Complete their dialogue.**

H: [1] .... a game of golf?

F: No thanks. I [2] ....

H: Oh, come on! [3] ....

F: But [4] .... for ages.

H: [5] ....

F: I haven't got any golf clubs.

H: [6] ....

F: Oh, all right. Just [7] ....

5 **Find eleven words to do with games and sports in the wordsquare.**

O	S	R	E	F	E	R	E	E	C
W	T	H	V	I	K	Y	P	A	H
I	O	D	S	H	U	F	F	L	E
N	R	B	O	A	R	D	W	J	R
N	P	A	G	E	V	I	R	S	U
E	L	N	S	T	L	C	H	C	L
R	C	K	A	T	H	L	A	O	E
J	W	E	R	P	F	R	M	R	S
U	H	R	D	L	G	Y	O	E	D
C	M	P	O	I	N	T	S	W	R

1 **Complete the dialogue between Tessa and Pete using the verbs in brackets in the correct tense.**

P: Of course if you .... *(get)* a cat, it .... *(be)* much cheaper to feed than a dog.
T: And it .... *(not take up)* so much room.
P: That's true. And cats .... *(be)* very independent animals. You .... *(not have)* any problems if you .... *(want)* to go out for the day. But what .... you .... *(do)* if you .... *(go away)* for more than a day?
T: If I .... *(ask)* my neighbours they .... *(look after)* it.
P: Oh, well that's all right then.

2 **What do you think is the best pet for these people? Give reasons for your choice.**

1

2

3

4

1 ....
2 ....
3 ....
4 ....

3 **Read the sentences and then number them to show the correct order.**

The next day and almost every day for the next nine years Hachiko returned to the station and waited for his master, who never came.

And every evening he met Dr Veno when he came back from his work at Tokyo University.

1 Hachiko the dog became famous for his loyalty in the 1920s and 1930s.

One day Dr Veno died while he was at work.

Every morning he went with his master, Dr Veno, to Shibuya railway station in Tokyo.

Hachiko waited for his master at the station until midnight.

A statue was erected to his memory at the place where he sat and waited.

9 Today it is a popular meeting point for friends in Shibuya.

Hachiko finally died in 1934 and by then he was famous throughout Japan.

4 **Complete the sentences.**

1 *If a cat catches a bird, it will play with it.*
2 If a dog sees a cat, ...
3 If a bird finds a worm, ...
4 If you don't frighten a snake, ...
5 If a zebra sees a lion, ...
6 If a dog doesn't like you, ...

5 **a** **Match the beginnings of these animal expressions in A with the correct endings in B.**

A	B
1 You can't teach an old dog	a but you can't make it drink.
2 You can lead a horse to water	b out of water.
3 (Someone) is like a bull	c in the grass.
4 (Someone) is like a fish	d in a china shop.
5 (Someone) is a snake	e before they are hatched.
6 Don't count your chickens	f new tricks.

b **Now write a sentence about each expression, to explain what you think it means. If you don't know, guess!**

1 ....
2 ....
3 ....
4 ....
5 ....
6 ....

Grammar reference

Unit 1

The present simple

1 You use the present simple most commonly to talk about:
a) regular or habitual actions.
I *go* to work every day.
b) facts
Toledo is a Spanish city.

2 ***Yes/no* questions: short answers**

Is	she/he	happy?	— Yes (No)	she/he is (isn't).	
Are	they		they are	(aren't).	

Do	you	live here?	— Yes (No)	I	do (don't).
Does	she/he		she/he	does	(doesn't).

Unit 2

Have/have got

1 *Have got* is often used instead of *have* in spoken British English. In written texts, *have* is more common.
'I'*ve got* an umbrella.'
Heathrow *has* four terminals.

2 *Have got* can also be used in questions, and can be answered using a short answer or an extended answer.
Have you got any brothers or sisters?
— Yes, I *have*. I'*ve got* two sisters.
Note that in the short answer, *have* is used rather than *have got*.

3 *Have got* is often less formal than *have*.
Do you have a ticket? Formal
Have you got any tickets left? Informal

Unit 3

The present continuous

1 The form of the present continuous is:

I	am	eating.
She/He	is	
You/We/They	are	

2 You use the present continuous to talk about:
a) something that is happening at the moment you are speaking.
What *are you doing*? — I'*m washing* my hair.
b) a temporary situation.
I *am collecting* money for a trip across Africa.
c) changes and development.
Their writing *is improving* all the time.

3 You often use a time expression when you want to show that you are talking about the present time.
She *is writing* a book *at the moment*.

Want to + infinitive

Certain verbs to do with hopes and wishes cannot be used in the present continuous, but take *to* + infinitive clause after the verb.
She *wants to be* comfortable.
Some other verbs which cannot be used in the present continuous tense include *hope*, *expect* and *wish*.

Unit 4

The past simple

1 The past simple is formed by adding *-ed* to the infinitive root.
start started
move moved
retire retired
See the irregular verbs table in the Teacher's Book for a list of common irregular verbs. See Unit 8 for the past simple in negatives and questions.

2 You use the past simple if you want to say:
a) that something happened in the past.
They *shared* rooms in Baker Street.
b) that something happened at a particular time in the past.
He *retired* in 1903.

Unit 5

Adverbs of frequency

1 You use an adverb of frequency to show how many times something happens.
She *often* goes to the cinema.

2 You can put the adverb in different positions but it is usually:
a) after the verb *to be*.
She *is always* happy.
They *aren't usually* late.
b) before other verbs.
He *rarely speaks* in the morning.
We *never eat* in restaurants.

Unit 6

Like + gerund

You use *like* + gerund if you are talking simply about likes and dislikes.

She *likes* work*ing* from home.
He *likes* go*ing* out.

Note that *would you like ...?* is always followed by an infinitive.

Would you like to come to the party?

Too and *very*

1 You use *too* to give something a negative meaning.

My feet are *too* big. (I can't find any shoes that fit me.)
It was *too* hot. (So we couldn't go out.)

2 You use *very* to emphasise something.

My feet are *very* big. (But I can still find shoes to wear.)
It was *very* hot. (But not too hot.)

Note that you cannot use *too* instead of *very*.

* I am too happy to meet you.
I am *very* happy to meet you.

Unit 7

Can for ability

You use *can* to say that someone has a skill or ability, or that they are able to do something. You use it followed by the base form of a verb.

I/You/She/He/We/They	can cannot/can't	swim.

Unit 8

The past simple in negatives and questions

See Unit 4 for uses of the past simple.

1 When making negatives and questions in the past, you use *did*. The main verb is in the infinitive.

Negative

I/You/He/She/We/They	did not/didn't	see him yesterday.

Question

Did	I/you/she/he/they	give him the money?

2 With the verb *to be*, *did* is not used in negatives and questions.

Negative

I/She/He You/We/They	was not/wasn't were not/weren't	at home last night.

Question

Was Were	I/she/he you/we/they	right?

Unit 9

The imperative

1 You use the imperative when you want:

a) to tell someone to do or not to do something.

Stop him!
Don't touch that!

b) to give advice or a warning.

Be careful.

2 Advice or warnings are often expressed in the negative.

Don't be afraid of them.
Don't go there. It's not very good.

3 The negative can also be formed by putting *never* in front of the base form of a verb.

Never open the door without looking.

Unit 10

The present continuous for future arrangements

See Unit 3 for present continuous form.

You can use the present continuous to talk about a particular time in the future. You can use a time expression to make it clear that you are talking about the future. This is not necessary when the event is understood to be in the future.

We*'re having* a meeting *on Thursday afternoon*.
— Who *is coming*?

Unit 11

How much...?/How many...?

You use *How many* with plural countable nouns, and *How much* with uncountable nouns. See Unit 17 for information on (un)countable nouns.

How many languages can you speak?
— Not many./Lots.
How much money did you spend on it?
— Not much./A lot.

Unit 12

Going to + infinitive for future plans

1 You use *going to* + infinitive to for your future plans and intentions.

I	'm/am	
She/He	's/is	going to get married next year.
You/We/They	're/are	

Questions

What	is	she/he	going to do?
	are	you/we/they	

Is	she/he	going to visit her?
	you/we/they	

2 You can use the present continuous instead of *going to* + infinitive, but this means that arrangements have been made.

My brother*'s* getting married next Saturday. (date given)
I'm not going to get married. (no special plans made yet)

Unit 13

Must, should and *can*

1 You use *must/must not* to say that:

a) something is requried by a rule or a law.
You *must* put your seatbelt on for take-off and landing.
You *mustn't* smoke during take-off.

b) something has to be done because you feel it is important.
You *must* come at once. Your house is on fire.

2 You use *should/should not:*

a) when you are advising someone to do/not to do something.
You *should* wash your hands before you eat.
You really *shouldn't* go out alone at night.

b) when you are saying that something is the right thing to do.
We *should* send her a postcard.

3 You use *can/cannot* to say that someone is allowed to/not allowed to do something.

You *can* go now.
You *cannot* go in there. It's private.

Note that this is not the same as *can* for ability. See Unit 7.

Unit 14

The present perfect

1 The form of the present perfect is:

I/You/We/They	have	visited many countries.
She/He	has	

Questions

Have	you/we/they	finished?
Has	she/he	

2 You use the present perfect for something that happened in the past but not at a specific time.

He *has been* to England.

It also connects a past action or event to the present.

I *have lived* in England all my life.

Unit 15

Comparative and superlative adjectives

1 Comparative adjectives consist of the adjective + *-er* for one or two syllable adjectives. When the adjective ends in a *y* this is changed to an *i*.

My brother is *younger* than me.
She is much *happier* than she was yesterday.

When the adjective is longer than two syllables, *more* is placed in front of it.

This book is *more interesting* than the last one I read.

2 Superlative adjectives consist of *the* + adjective + *-est* for one or two syllable adjectives. When the adjective ends in a *y* this is changed to an *i*.

He is *the richest* man in the country.
July is *the busiest* month at this hotel.

When the adjective is longer than two syllables, *most* is placed in front of it.

They are *the most famous* twins in history.

3 Irregular forms of comparative and superlative adjectives are:

good	better	best
bad	worse	worst

Unit 16

Future certainty and possibility

1 You use *will* and *won't* to talk about future certainty.

People *will have* more free time.
People *won't work* after the age of 50.

2 You use *might/might not* to talk about future possibility.

People *might visit* Mars.
He *might not arrive* on time.

Unit 17

Countable and uncountable nouns

1 You use countable nouns to refer to people or things that you can count. They have a plural form.

The mountains look beautiful.
The beaches are very clean.

They are usually preceded by a number or determiner (*a* or *the*).

2 You use uncountable nouns to refer to general things rather than objects. You cannot count them, and they do not have a plural form.

There was *food* for everybody in the hall.
The *scenery* was magnificent.

You do not use these nouns with numbers, but you can use expressions such as *some/a lot of.*

I need *some paper.*
There was *a lot of rain.*

There is/there are

You use *there is* and *there are* to talk about something that exists.

There is some magnificent scenery.
There are seven Land Rovers.

Unit 18

The present perfect continuous

1 You use the present perfect continuous to describe activities that started in the past, continued and are still happening now.

I/You/We/They	have/'ve	been saving up to go on
She/He	has/'s	holiday.

2 If you want to describe the duration of the event you use:

a) *for* to emphasise how long something lasts.
We *have been waiting for* an hour.

b) *since* to show when something started.
He's *been working* in London *since* January.

Unit 19

Have to + infinitive

1 *Have + to* and *must* have similar meanings. *Must* means there is a rule and *have to* usually means a rule you have made yourself.

You *must* put out your cigarettes.
= There is a rule which tells you to do this.
I *have to* stop smoking.
= I have decided to stop smoking.

Note that in the negative, their meanings are different.

You *must not* leave the room.
= You are not allowed to leave the room.
You *don't have to* leave the room.
= You can leave the room if you want to, but it is not necessary.

2 You can use *have to* to say that something is necessary or extremely important.

You *have to listen* carefully to understand what he says.

3 You can use *have to* without an infinitive if the infinitive is understood.

Why do you get up so early?
— I *have to.* I start work at eight.

Unit 20

When and *if* in the first conditional

1 You use the first conditional to describe something that is going to happen. There are two parts to the sentence. The first part describes the event and the second part describes the results of the event. In the first part of the sentence, *when* and *if* are followed by the present tense.

When you go to the shop	you won't know what to choose.
If he comes soon	we will catch the train.

2 You can reverse the order of the two parts of the sentence.

If it's fine tomorrow, we'*ll* go for a walk.
We'*ll* go for a walk *if* it's fine tomorrow.

3 You use *when* to show that you expect something to happen and *if* to show that something might/might not happen.

When I see her, I'*ll* tell her. (I know I will see her.)
If I see her, I'*ll* tell her. (I'm not sure that I will see her.)

Tapescripts

I = Interviewer **M** = Man **W** = Woman **B** = Boy

Unit 1

Exercise 2: Personal information

Part 1

W So, let's get a form and I can fill in a few personal details.
J Mhmm.
W Here we are. Now, first name, Jo-sette.
J That's right.
W I've got your address here. Just a moment. Now, what's your surname, Josette?
J Aparis.
W A-P-A-R-E ...?
J No, I. A-P-A-R-I-S.
W Right. And female. Now, what about your friend? Are you looking for a male or female friend, or either?
J Male. I have quite a lot of female friends, but I don't know many men here.
W OK. So your ideal friend is male. And you're French?
J That's right.
W Now, what about your friend's nationality?
J Oh, it doesn't matter. Er, well, I don't want French because I'm learning English here, so someone who speaks English.
W OK. So, any nationality but a native English speaker or a good English speaker.
J Yes.
W Right. What do you do, Josette?
J I'm a student.
W Student. And how old are you?
J 21.
W And your friend? Do you want someone the same age as you?
J Yes. Well, er, in his twenties.
W So, between twenty and thirty.
J Yes.
W Right. And how tall are you Josette ...?

Part 2

W Now, here you put your interests. For example, are you interested in travel, any particular sport ...
J Right. Er, that's OK. I'm interested in travel, not, er, in the theatre. So I put a tick here beside travel. Er, and what about this question here - music?
W Yes, what kind of music do you like? Do you like classical music, pop music ...
J Well, er, I like all kinds of music really.
W So, tick music and write 'all kinds of music' in the space.
J And here I describe myself?
W Yes, for example, are you shy or sociable, friendly, serious ...
J Oh dear. Er, I'm not sure. I'm quite serious, I suppose, but, er, not very shy.
W When you've finished, answer the question at the bottom. Do you smoke?
J Yes, I do.
W And what about your friend? Do you want someone who smokes or a non-smoker?
J Oh, it doesn't matter.
W OK. Just write 'not important' here. Then you sign at the bottom here ...

Exercise 6: Small talk

Dialogue A

M1 Hi!
M2 Hi. OK?
M1 Yeah. Fine. You?
M2 Not bad, thanks. See you.
M1 Yeah. Cheerio.

Dialogue B

M Well, thanks very much. That was very helpful. And it was very nice meeting you Mrs Cunningham.
W And you. And I look forward to our meeting next month in New York. Goodbye, Mr Stevens.
M Goodbye.

Dialogue C

B1 Dad, this is Michael. Michael, my father.
B2 How do you do, Mr Barnes?
M I'm very pleased to meet you, Michael.
B1 And this is my sister, Theresa.
B2 Pleased to meet you, Theresa.
W Hello.
M Well, sit down, Michael. Here, let me take your coat.

Dialogue D

M1 Good morning, Janet.
W Good morning. Cold today, isn't it?
M2 Yes, freezing. Good morning, Bob.
M1 Morning. How are you?
M2 Fine, thanks.
M1 Good. Janet. Have you got those letters ...?

Dialogue E

W1 Goodnight.
W2 Goodnight, Yvonne. Thanks for a lovely meal.
M Yes, it was really nice. Thanks a lot.
W1 Glad you enjoyed it. See you on Friday.
M Yes. OK. Goodnight.
W2 Bye.
W1 Night.

Unit 2

Exercise 2: A home of my own

Dialogue A

I Who do you live with, Willem?
W With two friends.
I And do you live in Amsterdam, or near Amsterdam?
W We live in an old windmill about twenty kilometres from Amsterdam.
I A windmill! Really?
W Yes, the three of us bought it two years ago and we all worked together to put in a kitchen and a bathroom and so on.
I You did the work yourselves?
W Yes, most of it. Someone helped us build new floors and ceilings, but we did about 80% of the work ourselves.
I That's really good.
W Yes. We love it. And it's very comfortable now with a proper kitchen, living room and everyone has got their own bedroom. But we haven't got any electricity or central heating yet.

Dialogue B

I Hiro, you live in Japan, don't you?
H That's right. I've got my own flat near the centre.
I What's your flat like? Is it a modern one?
H Yes. It's in a modern block. It's small - most flats in Tokyo are very small. Mine has got one room and a very small kitchen. It's tiny really, and it hasn't got a bathroom, just a toilet.
I So where do you have a bath?
H In the public baths on my street. A lot of people in Tokyo use the public baths.
I And the living room and bedroom are the same room?
H That's right. And outside the living room there's a balcony. I grow lots of plants on the balcony. It's small, but I like it a lot.

Dialogue C

I Whereabouts in France do you live, Florence?
F In the north, in a small village called Duclair.
I Do you live by yourself?
F No, with my family - even my grandparents live with us!
I So what's your house like? I suppose it's quite big if all the family live there.
F Yes, it's very big.
I How many bedrooms has it got?
F Seven, but we need them all because I've got two brothers and two sisters. Then there's me, my parents and grandparents. My grandparents have their own kitchen and bathroom.
I So it's got two kitchens and two bathrooms?
F No - three bathrooms! One for my grandparents, one for my parents and one for the children. Yes, it is a huge old house and it's got a beautiful garden at the back. I love it.
I And you've got your own bedroom?
F Yes, it's in the attic at the top of the house.

Exercise 5: Designs on a room

ID Now, I designed this bedroom last year. It's quite similar in shape and size to yours.
M Mhmm. It looks bigger than mine. It's very nice.
ID Yes. The colours and the space in the middle make it look bigger. But it was about five metres by five.
M What's that? About fifteen feet by fifteen?
ID Yes. You see it's a square room, like yours. And I put the table here, under the window for maximum light.
M Mhmm.
ID And the bed against this wall, opposite the door. You see, this wall had no doors or radiators or anything so we had the length of the wall for the bed and at each side the two fitted wardrobes.
M Yes. They look very nice, and I need a lot of storage space.
ID That's right. These wardrobes have got a lot space inside.
M Mhmm. And what about drawers? There isn't a chest of drawers in the room.
ID No. The wardrobes have got a set of drawers inside. You see, if we put nearly all the furniture along this wall there is much more space in the room. And, as you can see, the whole room is decorated in very pale colours which make it look bigger. And for a splash of colour, I put this very colourful Chinese rug in the middle of the room.
M Yes. It looks lovely.
ID Now, this one is quite different. It's much more colourful and ...

Unit 3

Exercise 4: Dreams come true

DJ So let's hear some ambitions for the New Year and tell us what you're doing to realise these ambitions. Ambitions big or small, let's hear from you. OK, Sue. Go ahead.
S Hello.
DJ Hello, Sue. So what's your ambition for this year?
S To go to Hong Kong.
DJ How old are you, Sue?
S 18.
DJ And why Hong Kong? Have you got friends there?
S No. I've seen lots of pictures of Hong Kong and it looks fantastic. I just want to go.
DJ That's quite an expensive trip.
S I know. So, I'm working in a factory at the moment to save the money. I'm packing boxes nine hours a day, six days a week.
DJ And are you enjoying it?
S No, definitely not. But I'm saving money and next month I'll have enough money to buy the ticket - I hope.
DJ Well, all the best, Sue, and I hope you have a great time in Hong Kong. And next on the line is Alan. Hello, Alan.
A Hello, Dave. You want to know my ambition?
DJ We certainly do.
A I'm running twenty miles every day at the moment

because I want to enter for the New York Marathon next year.
DJ I admire you, Alan. Do you think you've got the right experience?
A Oh, yes. I ran in the London Marathon last year and I did quite well, so I want to make the New York one this year.
DJ And how's the training going?
A Fine, but I'm losing a lot of weight right now so I'm watching my diet very carefully.
DJ Well, all the best, Alan. And don't overdo it. Now we've got Matthew ready to talk to us. Matthew, can you tell us your ambition for this year?
M Hello. Yes, well, this is something I've wanted to do for a long time. I want to pass my driving test before my fortieth birthday.
DJ Do you need to learn to drive for your job?
M Oh, no. I just want to do it for myself.
DJ Well, when is your fortieth birthday?
M In two years time.
DJ Two years? You've got plenty of time.
M Well, not really. You see I've been trying for fifteen years now and I've failed seventeen times.
DJ Oh dear.
M I know. It's terrible. I'm having lessons every day now. I've got my test next month and I'm already feeling nervous.
DJ Well, the best of luck, Matthew. I'll keep my fingers crossed ...

Exercise 6: A driving ambition

R Good morning, Peak Driving School.
S Oh, good morning. I'm phoning about driving lessons.
R Yes ...
S The thing is my father's teaching me, but I want to have some lessons from a school as well. Is that possible?
R Certainly. You have a test lesson with us so we can see how you drive, and then we tell you how many more lessons you need.
S I see ... and how much does each lesson cost?
R Fifteen pounds fifty for one hour.
S Right, could I book the test lesson then, please?
R Yes of course. Er, how about next Wednesday at four o'clock?
S Wednesday at four ... yes, that's fine.
R And could I have your name and address, please?
S Sarah Jones, 12 Station Road.
R Thank you Miss Jones. Goodbye.
S Thanks, goodbye.

Unit 4

Exercise 2: Elementary, my dear Watson!

I My guest today, Alison Thomas, has just written a book about one of the greatest detectives of all time, Sherlock Holmes. Alison, can you tell us a bit about your book?
A Certainly. It's about his life. I'm most interested in what happened to him after he gave up his detective work. We know a lot about Sherlock Holmes, the detective, but we don't really know what happened to him after that. He retired at quite an early age, you know. He was only about fifty.
I So what did he do after he retired?
A Well, that's the interesting thing, nobody really knows.
I Perhaps he got tired and wanted to lead a quiet life?
A Maybe, but I don't think so. Some people think that he became a spy. I think he continued to work because he was such an active and energetic person - not really the kind of person to retire early. He probably worked for the government in some way. He knew a lot of famous people and he had an active mind. Other people think he retired just to study bees, but I'm not so sure.
I Perhaps he got married.
A Oh, no. I'm sure he didn't. He wasn't interested in marriage. No, I don't think he got married and I don't think he retired.
I So what about his earlier life ...

Exercise 4: The Woman in Black

The man and the woman were husband and wife. Twenty years ago the woman had run away with another man. She wanted everyone to believe she was dead. So before she disappeared, she sent a note to the police to say she thought her husband wanted to kill her and that she was very scared.The next day she shot off two of her fingers and left them in the garden. The police came to the house, found the woman had disappeared and found her fingers in the garden. They arrested the husband for murder and he spent the next twenty years in prison. The day the man got on the train to Vienna was the day of his release from prison. He had only his old clothes which he wore the day he was arrested. That's why they looked very old-fashioned. When he got on the train, he thought he recognised the woman but he couldn't see her face because of the veil. As soon as she took off her gloves, he was sure it was his wife. He jumped up, told the woman who he was and strangled her. People in the train heard the noise and came rushing to the compartment but too late, he had murdered his wife. The police arrested him, but when they found it was the man who had just been in prison for the last twenty years for his wife's murder, they released him because he had already had his punishment.

Unit 5

Exercise 5: A dancer's diet

I Gill, as a professional dancer, are you very careful about what you eat?
G Not at all. I eat what I want, really. Although I never have lunch because I'm always too busy practising. I just drink lots of water during the day. But I usually have quite a big breakfast.
I What do you have?
G Oh, cereal with milk or yoghurt, toast, maybe one or

two pieces, with jam, cheese or sometimes a boiled egg. I never eat butter, though, only margarine.

I And for dinner?

G A normal meal. Er - fish, chips, vegetables or chicken, rice er, pasta and sauce. Something like that. Not much red meat, more fish or chicken. I suppose I eat lots of fruit and raw vegetables, like salad and grated carrots. I know some dancers who never eat anything fattening. I have a friend, for example. She nearly kills herself trying to stay thin. I don't agree with that.

I What kind of things does she eat, then?

G Oh, er lemon tea for breakfast. She never eats anything in the morning. Then maybe a carrot at lunchtime and she usually has a bit of plain yoghurt and lemon juice for dinner. On Sunday she sometimes has a piece of grilled chicken and salad. But that's all.

I Goodness. That's not very much!

G No. I was like that myself a few years ago. I watched every little thing I ate and I only weighed about 40 kilos, but I often felt sick at the end of the day. I'm fine now. I'm never sick.

Exercise 6: Offering food and drink

Dialogue A

W How about a drink?

M Yes, please. I'll have a beer.

W They don't sell beer here! It's all mineral water and carrot juice!

M Oh, sorry, I forgot. I'll have an orange juice then, please.

W Ice?

M Yes, please.

W Anything to eat?

M No, not just now thanks.

Dialogue B

Wa Would you like tea or coffee, madam?

W I'll have coffee, please.

Wa Sir?

M Er, tea for me please ... thanks.

Wa Cream or milk, madam?

W Neither, thank you.

Wa Sir?

M Have you got any lemon?

Wa Certainly, sir. Here you are.

M That's great. Thank you.

Unit 6

Exercise 4: Position vacant

M In this advert here it says 'Experienced cook wanted'. What does 'experienced' mean?

W It means, er, they've done this job before. This is not their first job as a cook so they know a lot about cooking.

M Right. I see. And what about this word? In this advert about tour guides. It says 'No qualifications necessary'. Can you explain the meaning of 'qualifications'?

W Er, it's the same as exams or diplomas. So 'no qualifications' means you don't need to have passed any exams to do this job.

M OK. Thanks. I understand it now.

W Anything else?

M No, thanks. Everything else is fine.

Exercise 6: Unusual jobs

Dialogue A

I Andrew, your job is quite unusual for a man, isn't it?

A Not really. There are a lot of male models. But I suppose being a model is more popular with women than men.

I And you enjoy your job?

A I love it. I'm lucky to earn money from something I really enjoy. And I enjoy training too.

I Training?

A Well, yes. We have to keep fit, eat well, you know to keep looking good. But I like weight training and I love swimming and walking, so it's no problem for me.

I And do you earn a lot?

A I can earn £500 a day, but there are some days, of course, when I don't have any work. That's what I don't like. I hate waiting for the phone to ring, waiting for that next job. But I like working hard for a few days and then having a few days off. But one problem is you sometimes have to do quite dangerous jobs.

I Dangerous?

A Yes. One time I nearly killed myself when I had to do a job skiing down a mountain. There was an avalanche and I'm not even a good skier. I was scared I can tell you. So I don't like doing dangerous jobs but most jobs are OK. No, usually it's good fun and I love travelling and I've been to some interesting places.

Dialogue B

I Jason, you have a very unusual job. Can you tell me something about it?

J Yes, well, I'm a busker, or street entertainer. So I bring my music here to the Square and dance. I love dancing so it's a great job for me. But I don't like coming out in the bad weather, you know, if it's too cold or too wet. So I do most of my work in spring and summer. Lots of people come in the summer, and if they like my dancing they put money in the hat. My partner takes the hat round during the show. Some people give a lot, some just a few pence.

I Do you get a lot of money?

J Some days I do. In the summer, I can get over a hundred a day.

I A hundred pounds a day?

J Yes, maybe more. But next year I'm going to try in Paris. It's too difficult here with the police, sometimes. Like - I don't like thinking about the police all the time - you know, are they going to tell me I'm making too much noise, that kind of thing. People tell me it's much better in Paris.

I Well, all the best. I think you're a great dancer.

J Thanks.

Unit 7

Exercise 5: Can you read Japanese?

I Hiro, can you tell us something about the Japanese language? It looks so difficult to read and write.
H Yes. It's not really difficult.
I But there are so many characters or symbols. How can you learn them all?
H Well, there are a lot of characters in the Japanese language. Maybe about five or six thousand but nobody knows all of them.
I How many do you know?
H About two thousand. But I was a university student, so I can do more than some people. For example, when you leave secondary school you should know about eight hundred then you can read most things.
I So children learn them slowly at school?
H That's right. They just learn a few every week.
I But how can young children read books if they only know a few characters? You mean they can only begin to read books when they are about fourteen years old?
H No. There are lots of books for children but we have another alphabet, a very simple one, that children learn first.
I Another alphabet?
H Yes. It's called Hiragana.
I How does it work?
H Well, for example, I come from Yokohama in Japan so my town has four sounds: yo-ko-ha-ma. And there is one Japanese letter for yo, one for ko, one for ha and one for ma, so yo-ko-ha-ma has four letters. There are about 46 basic letters and each one is a Japanese sound.
I So that's called Hir-, er Hira?
H Hiragana.
I What do you call the other system - the difficult one?
H It's called Kanji.
I And Kanji is from Chinese, isn't it?
H That's right. Yes. About two thousand years ago, people couldn't write Japanese and then they learned the Chinese writing system and used the Chinese characters to write Japanese words. So we write the same as the Chinese but we say it differently.

Exercise 6: Code cracking

M What's this? 'Cracking the Code'. What do we do?
W Well, these numbers are instead of letters. We find which number is which letter.
M So, maybe 1 is A and 2 is B and so on.
W Let's try that. Mhmm. No. That can't be right. Look, 2426, B - a, b, c, d, D. BDB, - a, b, c, d, e, f, F. BDBF? That's wrong.
M Let's try 24, 26. Er, that's, er X and Z. X and Z? No, that can't be right!
W I know. Why don't we try it backwards? 1 is Z, not A. So A is 26, B is 25, C is 24. Like that.
M OK. Let's try. So, 24 is C. 26 is A. CA? What's that?
W Let's go on to the next letter. 13? What's that?
M Er, I know. Why don't we write down all the alphabet and then write down the numbers on top and go backwards with Z as 1, Y as 2, X as 3 and so on.
W Yes. That's a good idea. Let's try that.

Unit 8

Exercise 5: The roaring twenties

I And you were alive then, weren't you?
M Yes, of course, I was very young, but I was alive!
I And you remember the 1920s?
M Oh, yes. I remember, so many things happened. There was something new nearly every day. Everyone started to listen to the radio, and then the first television came out and - cars. Do you know that in 1919 there were 7 million cars in the USA, but by 1929 there were 23 million? Oh, it was fantastic, really. Every week another family got a car. People started flying across the world. Oh, everything changed very quickly. I can remember our family getting its first fridge and washing machine. We thought we were so modern!
I So most people in the States became much richer?
M Well, the rich became very, very rich, and our family did OK at first. But there were still a lot of poor people. Oh, no. Not ... not everyone was rich. But we thought that if we waited a few more years then everyone could, you know er, even the poor people could get rich. But, of course, that didn't happen.
I Do you remember the Wall Street Crash in 1929?
M Oh, yes I do. A terrible time.
I Many families lost everything, didn't they?
M Yes. Our family too. My father's business collapsed. We lost everything. We sold our house, car, even the washing machine went. Oh yes. People lost thousands, millions of dollars.
I And millions of people lost their jobs, didn't they?
M Yes, I think it was 13 or 14 million in America who didn't have jobs in 1930 and millions of others with only part-time jobs. And of course it was the same in Europe. Oh yes it was a ... a terrible end to a decade. Rich one minute, poor the next.

Unit 9

Exercise 3: Green maze

Speaker A

Take the second turning on the left, turn right after the statue, then turn left. Turn left again, and the exit is on your right.

Speaker B

Take the third turning on the right, then turn left. Turn right before the fountain and then take the first turning on your right. Take the second turning on the left and the exit is straight ahead.

Exercise 5: Right or wrong?

Dialogue A

M What do you think about using animals for sport?
W I don't agree with it. It's wrong.
M Why do you say that?
W Well, look at dog fighting, for example. Some people organise dog fights where the dogs kill each other and people do it just to win money on, you know, the best fighter.

M Yes, that's wrong, I agree.
W Even insects. Do you know some people organise fights between insects? They just watch one insect killing another and bet money on the fight.
M Do you think that's wrong? I mean, dogs are one thing but insects? They don't really feel anything, do they?
W That's not true. I think it's wrong to do that to any animal.
M Mhmm?

Dialogue B

M What do you think about this? It says here that in Japan they can make cars which don't need petrol.
W Yeah? What do they use, then?
M I can't explain it exactly, but they use a gas which comes from burning rubbish. I think it's a really good idea. They burn rubbish and then they collect the gas, you know, that comes off, and then use it to make fuel for car engines.
W Well, that sounds a good idea. It's probably cheaper than petrol too.
M Mhmm, mhmm. And it says it gives 25% more power than other fuels.

Dialogue C

M Don't you find them very expensive?
W Yes, they are, but it's much easier than washing them every day. But you're right, they're very expensive, really.
M Babies make so much rubbish, don't they?
W Very true! And all this plastic. It's very difficult to get rid of plastic rubbish, you know.
M Yes, I know. Don't you think they could make them without all that plastic?
W Well, I believe they can now but we haven't got them in the supermarkets yet.

Unit 10

Exercise 3: Booking a place

R Quality Hotel. Good afternoon.
V Oh, hello. I'm telephoning about the Murder Weekends. I'd like to book a room for myself and my husband.
R OK. Now when would you like to come?
V A week on Friday.
R So you want a double room for Friday and Saturday night, the 13th and 14th?
V Yes, thanks.
R What name is it, please?
V Valentine. Mr and Mrs Valentine.
R Mr and Mrs Valentine. Now, would you like a room with a balcony overlooking the garden?
V Er, no thanks. Just a standard room.
R Right. And dinner on Friday evening?
V No, I don't think so. What time do you begin, er with the murder story?
R After dinner on Friday evening. Dinner is at seven thirty, so about eight thirty to nine. It's better to be here by half past eight, really.
V That's fine. We're catching the five thirty train from Cardiff, so we should be in Swindon by about eight. How far are you from the station?
R It's about three miles so if you're not coming by car, you'll need to get a taxi. The hotel has a taxi service from the station. I can book that for you.
V Can I book one now?
R Certainly, madam. What time does your train get into Swindon?
V Five past eight.
R Right. So there'll be a taxi waiting for you and you'll be here about half past eight.
V Half past eight. Fine. And I believe you can hire fancy dress costumes at the hotel?
R That's right. You can hire them when you get here. Do you need costumes for both of you?
V No, just for me. My husband's bringing his own clothes.
R That's fine. So let me just go over the details. A double room for Mr and Mrs Valentine, no balcony. You don't need dinner Friday evening and you want a taxi at the station for five past eight ...

Exercise 5: Going out

Dialogue A

M Look. There's a walk round the city on Sunday morning. Would you like to go?
W What time does it start?
M Half past eight.
W Half past eight? On Sunday morning? Oh, no. That's too early for me. No thanks. I don't think so.
M Oh, come on. Just one Sunday. It looks interesting. It's a historic walk round old churches, and prisons. Why don't you come?
W Oh, all right. Just this once.

Dialogue B

W I've got two tickets for the ballet on Friday. Would you like to come with me?
M Yes. I'd love to. What time does it begin?
W Seven forty five.
M So, shall we meet at seven?
W Yes, where?
M How about outside the theatre?
W Great. See you there at seven on Friday.

Dialogue C

M Oh, er, hello Susan. This is Maurice.
W Hello, Maurice. What do you want?
M Well, er, there's a very good Spanish film on at the moment. I thought, maybe you'd like to come with me one ... one evening.
W No. I'm afraid I can't, Maurice. I'm quite busy at the moment.
M Well, what about next week? We could go then, if you're not too busy.
W No, I'm afraid I haven't got much time in the next three months, Maurice. Sorry. Oh, there's someone at the door. I'll have to go. Bye, Maurice.

Exercise 6: Activity weekends

W Right. Can we just take a few minutes to tell you about some of the arrangements this weekend. Maggie?
Ma For those of you who don't know me, my name's Maggie and I'm taking the walkers and sightseers. On Saturday morning we're going to the castle and gardens. We're meeting outside and we're going by minibus to the castle - leaving at ten. After we've looked round the castle and gardens we're walking back along footpaths and country roads. It's about 15 kilometres so bring comfortable shoes. It's not a difficult walk but it is quite long and it can be very muddy.
W Thanks, Maggie. Ian?
I OK. Well, on Saturday morning I'm taking the pottery class. This is a beginners class, so don't worry if you've never done it before. We're starting after breakfast at nine thirty in room 8. The class will last all morning, and if you're very keen, there's another class in the afternoon.
W Thanks, Ian. And now, Chris.
C Right. Well, for you sports people, we've got golf all day Sunday. We're meeting outside in the car park at ten and we're walking from here to the golf course. It's about a couple of miles so we'll be on the course at about ten thirty. And one more thing. I'm sorry but there's no parachuting today. I'm afraid it's too windy and they're not flying today. If it's better tomorrow we'll organise something then. I'll tell you about that at breakfast tomorrow. Right. That's it, I think.

Unit 11

Exercise 2: Youth enterprise

Part 1

I Youth Enterprise is a great opportunity for you and other school students. It's a chance for you to start a business for yourself while you are still at school. You work out your own ideas, make your own decisions and work together, as a business team. And don't forget, at the end there is a competition to find the best Youth Enterprise business in the country. The winners receive a cheque for £1,000, and there are two other prizes of £750 and £500 for the second and third teams. Now, are there any questions?

Part 2

S1 How many schools are there in the scheme?
I Well, last year there were about 2,000 schools in the scheme.
S2 And were they successful? I mean, did anyone make a profit?
I Oh, yes. There are some students here who had two very successful businesses.
S3 How much money do we get to start the business?
I You don't get any money. You have to find all the money yourselves. That's part of the competition.
S4 And you said we work in teams. How many people are there in a team?
I That depends. If there is a large group of you who can work together, then you can have a large team. But, er, if you prefer to work with a couple of friends, that's OK. It really depends on you and what you think will work the best. And we suggest you spend about two hours a week on the scheme. We don't want you to miss your other school work.
S5 And can we get advice from anyone?
I Yes. There is a teacher in each school who can help you. If you think it's helpful the teacher can ask one of our advisers to come to the school to answer more questions. And now I'd like to introduce Brian and David who can tell you about the business they started last year.

Part 3

I So, any questions for Brian and David?
S1 Er, what did you make?
B We made two things. The first thing was ties. Very colourful ties were really popular last year at school so we thought that was a good idea ...
D Yes, and the other thing was exam revision papers. We looked at a lot of exam papers from past years and made lots of very simple revision sheets in different subjects. They sold like hot cakes.
S2 How many ties did you sell?
D So far we've sold 400 and we have got orders for more.
S3 And how much profit did you make?
B With the ties and the revision papers together we made £500 profit last year.
S4 How much did the revision papers cost?
B £1.50 each. There were about 18 pages in each little booklet.
S5 How many students were there in the team?
D Er, eight. No, nine.
S1 And did you find that once you'd ...?

Exercise 6: Sympathising and congratulating

Part 1

Dialogue A

M How are things?
W Not too good, I'm afraid. Last week I only had ten customers. I made a loss of about £500.
M Oh, dear. I'm very sorry to hear that.

Dialogue B

W Hey, I've just won first prize in a competition!
M That's fantastic! What did you win?
W A holiday in the Bahamas.
M How wonderful!

Dialogue C

M I passed!
W Oh well done! Congratulations!
M Thanks. I got 68%.

Dialogue D

W What's wrong?
M Oh, we can't go the concert.
W Why not?
M They've sold out of tickets.
W Oh, no. What a pity. Never mind. We can go somewhere else.

Part 2

1 I passed my driving test.
2 We can't go on our picnic. The weather's too bad.
3 I've just won £700 in the lottery.
4 I got the job.
5 I'm afraid I didn't pass. I only got 30%.
6 I'm sorry I can't come tomorrow. My mother's in hospital.
7 We sold twelve paintings this week. We've made about £2,500.
8 I'm afraid we had to close down our business. We couldn't pay back the bank and we were making a loss.

Unit 12

Exercise 4: Different traditions

I So, what are you going to wear?
W Oh, it's a beautiful dress. The material came from India - my Aunt sent it to me. It's red and green with gold threads running through it. My mother's going to make it into a sari.
I You're not going to wear white then?
W Oh, no. Indian women can't wear white for weddings. In Indian tradition white means death, so it's for funerals.
I Oh, I see. So what's the usual colour for wedding dresses?
W Red or pink often with some green, as well. Red is a very important colour for weddings.
I Yes, I've seen women with their hands painted red. Is that henna?
W Yes it is. We use henna to paint patterns all over our hands.
I Are you going to do that?
W Oh yes. Well, my friends are going to paint them for me the night before the wedding.
I Mhmm. I think it looks lovely.
W Yes. And gold - that's another important colour at Indian weddings.
I Oh?
W Oh yes. My dress is going to have gold in it and I'm going to wear lots of gold jewellery, for example.
I Is that usual?
W Yes. The bride's parents buy her gold before the wedding. And we give presents that are gold too.
I What do you mean - you give presents? I thought the bride receives the presents not gives the presents?
W Well, it's Indian tradition. The bride's family gives presents to the bridegroom's mother, sister, uncle. Oh, all sorts of people get presents.
I What kind of presents?
W Jewellery, gold usually or sometimes money.
I So, you're going to buy lots of jewellery in the next few weeks for your husband's family?
W Yes, me and my Mum are going shopping tomorrow.
I I hope you're going to get some presents, too.
W Oh, yes! We get gold and money, too.

Exercise 6: Do you agree?

Dialogue A

W1 I think 18 is too young to get married.
M Yes, definitely.
W2 Well, I disagree. I got married at 17 and we're very happy.

Dialogue B

W I don't believe in marriage. I think if you love each other you don't need to get married.
M Oh, I don't think so. If you're married, you stay together longer.
W Yes, but if you love each other you stay together, too.
M No. I don't agree. It's not the same.

Dialogue C

W1 I think it's better to get married when you're between 25 and 30.
W2 Yes, I think so, too.
W1 You're not ready when you're young and you need to meet a lot of people before you choose someone you want to marry.
W2 Yes, that's right.

Dialogue D

M Well, I want to marry someone a few years younger than me.
W What? You think it's better for the man to be a bit older than the woman?
M Yes, I think so.
W No. It doesn't matter which one is older.

Unit 13

Exercise 2: Experienced travellers

Dialogue A

M Well, I know that everyone goes to see the pyramids but what else do you think we should see?
W Oh, in Cairo you should go to the museum. And I really enjoyed going round the mosques. Some of them are very beautiful.
M What else did you like?
W Oh, shopping in the bazaar. That was great. You should definitely go to the bazaar. There are some wonderful things and you sit down at the stall, drink tea and talk about how much you want to pay and ...
M What? They don't have fixed prices?
W Not really. You should bargain for things.
M Oh, I'm not sure I'd be very good at that. But what about food? What's Egyptian food like?
W Good. I like it. You should try some of the Egyptian restaurants and don't eat in your hotel all the time.
M Mhmm. So, what about the rest of the country ...

Dialogue B

W So when do you think is the best time to go?
M Well, winter's no good because it's too cold and the days are very short, you know, it gets dark in the middle of the afternoon. The best time is summer - between May and September. It's lovely then.

W And where did you stay when you went? In youth hostels?
M Mhmm.
W What are they like?
M Oh they are fantastic over there. There's a hostel in Stockholm that's in an old sailing ship.
W Really?
M Yes. But don't just go along without booking. You should always book in advance because they get really busy in summer.
W And can I book from here?
M Yes. Er, I've got the address of the tourist board somewhere ...

Dialogue C

M And do I need a visa?
W Yes, you must have a visa. And you should apply about two months before you go.
M So you think I should go at the end of summer?
W Yes. I think September and October are the best months. It's still warm, it's usually dry and sunny and the trees and parks are beautiful in October.
M So what clothes do I need then?
W Oh, cotton trousers and shirts, a sweater for the evenings and maybe one jacket but it's quite warm in the daytime.
M But was it difficult finding your way around? I mean, how can you read the signs?
W There are a lot of signs in the Roman alphabet in the big cities and in the tourist places they have signs in English. But people are very friendly and helpful and a lot of people can speak some English ...

Exercise 6: Money matters

Dialogue A

M Can I have £1,000 worth of traveller's cheques, please?
W Certainly, sir. Do you want the cheques in US dollars?
M Yes, please. And I'd like to change £500 into Hong Kong dollars, as well.
W Right. Could you sign here, please and I'll get you the Hong Kong dollars.

Dialogue B

W Here's my room key. Er, how much do I owe you?
M Thank you, madam. I'll just get your bill. That's 480 francs.
W Can I pay by credit card?
M I'm afraid we don't accept credit cards, just cash or cheques.
W Oh dear. Well, can you cash me these traveller's cheques, please?
M Certainly, madam. How much would you like?
W Er, £200 sterling in French francs.
M Right.

Dialogue C

W Hello. Can you change these German marks into pounds for me?
M Yes. I can change the notes but I'm afraid we can't change coins.
W Oh. Well, where can I change them?
M You can't change them - use them for your next holiday!

Unit 14

Exercise 4: Talented children

I And is it very difficult for the teachers, having a boy in the class who's so talented at maths?
W Well, it is in many ways. I mean, we've taught him everything we can - in maths. You see, he's only nine and he's passed exams for sixteen-year-olds.
I Really?
W Yes, but fortunately, his father helps us a lot. He was a maths teacher himself and he gives Ricardo extra maths problems to do. And his father has bought him a computer, so he can do a lot of extra work at home.
I Do you think that his parents and his teachers push him too hard?
W No, I don't think so. You see, he loves maths, and when he's finished one problem, he's looking for the next.

I Stephen is a very special boy, isn't he?
M Yes, he is. In many ways he doesn't have the normal abilities for a boy of his age. It's very difficult for him to read and write, for example.
I And he's sixteen now?
M That's right, and many eight-year-old boys can do much more than he can but, of course, he has a special talent.
I In drawing.
M Yes, he has always been fantastic at it. Stephen can look at any building for about five minutes and then draw it perfectly.
I Tell us about some of the drawings he's done.
M Well, he's drawn some very complex buildings likes the Doge's Palace in Venice. He's drawn the Gum department store in Moscow and the Kremlin, and they are wonderful. Famous art experts have looked at the drawings and said that Stephen's an excellent artist.
I And he just looks at these buildings for a few minutes and then draws them?
M That's right. It's very strange, isn't it. He has such a special talent in one thing, but he finds other things difficult.

Exercise 6: Checking understanding

Dialogue A

M Do you mean he scored over 1,000 goals?
W Yes, 1,200 I think.
M And he won three World Cup medals?
W Yes - in 1958, 1962 and 1970.
M Amazing.

Dialogue B

W What did you say? He wrote music when he was six years old?
M That's right.
W I can't believe it.
M It's true.
W And let me just check this. He wrote 1,000 pieces of music.
M Yes.
W Phew!

Unit 15

Exercise 4: Identical twins

I Now, Martin and Peter, you're identical twins, aren't you?
M Yes.
P That's right.
I And did your parents always know who was Martin and who was Peter?
P Yes, our parents did, but other people didn't. You know, I pretended I was Martin and he pretended he was me - especially with the teachers at school.
I I can imagine. And Martin, you were born first, weren't you?
M Yes, I was. Ten minutes before Peter.
I Do you think that's important?
M Yes, I'm bossier than my brother, more aggressive. I like to be, you know, always the first.
I Is that true, Peter?
P Yes, it is. I was always the quiet one and Martin was noisier than me as a child. And he liked to be the first in the class, you know, get the best marks.
I But you're different now, aren't you?
M Er, mhmm, yes. But I think Peter is still quieter than me.
I And you both had problems learning to speak, didn't you?
P Yes. It was difficult for our parents, really.
M Yes, you see, we had our own language. We didn't speak, you know, normally. We spoke in a special language to each other.
I So you and Peter could understand each other but nobody else could understand you?
P That's right. We were together all the time, so we spoke our own private language and we didn't need to learn to speak properly.
I Yes, I believe a lot of twins do this, have their own private language. Can you remember any of the language now?
M No, but Mum says we didn't say 'mum' or 'mummy', we called her 'Gobu'. My dad was 'Lotta' and we always said 'tek' if we wanted to say 'no'. I wish we had a cassette of us talking when we were babies. It would be really interesting now.

Unit 16

Exercise 4: Looking to the future

Dialogue A

M It says here that in fifty years time most people will work from home and we'll send our work to a central office by computer.
W Oh, I hope not.
M Why? I think it's quite a good idea to work from home.
W Oh, no. I don't think so. I like working with other people, not on my own.

Dialogue B

W Listen to this. 'By the year 2000 most homes will be heated by solar energy.'
M I hope so. I think it's the cheapest and cleanest form of energy.
W Yes, I think so too.

Dialogue C

W Do you know that in a hundred years time we'll all have robots to do the housework?
M Well, I hope so.
W Great idea, isn't it?
M What about our jobs? I hope we won't have robots to do our jobs as well.
W Oh no, I don't think so. Do you?
M Well, I hope not.

Exercise 6: Food for the future

Good morning. Today I'm going to talk about food - food in the future. Now, maybe some of you know this, but about two thirds of the world is covered by water - oceans, seas, lakes and so on. Two thirds of our planet is water, but most of our food comes from the land. Only two or three per cent of our food comes from oceans and seas. Now, we won't have enough food for everyone until we use the world's water better, more efficiently. Look at this illustration here. I want to show you how fishing could be much better in the future. We might have automatic fishing boats, for example, with computers and satellites telling the boats where to fish. But if we take out more fish from the sea we'll need to put something back. It won't be possible just to take more from the sea. So we'll have lots more fish farms producing fish all the time, to put the fish back into the sea.
Then there are vegetables. It's possible to have large vegetable farms on the sea. Like this illustration here. Vegetables on raised platforms in the sea. They won't use salt water of course, they'll use the water that comes off the sea in water vapour, as the sea gets warm.
Now, what about the desert? So much of our land is desert. But look at my illustrations of these large domes in the desert with pipes bringing water. The plants will get plenty of sun and the domes will keep the water inside. And then, who knows, we might have robots to plant, pick and pack the plants - a type of robotic farmer. And all these things will run on solar energy, of course. We will have solar energy everywhere in a few years time. Any questions so far ...?

Unit 17

Exercise 4: Adventurous ideas

I Sally, you've been in the travel business for a long time. How did it all start?
S Oh, I suppose when I was a child. You see, we lived in many different countries, er, first Britain, then Belgium, France, Spain and Switzerland.
I So you speak quite a lot of languages?

S Yes, French, Spanish, German and English. So, you see, I've been a traveller for a long time.
I So you decided to sell unusual holidays, adventure holidays, really.
S That's right.
I Can you tell us about some of the holidays we can get through your agency?
S Yes. Well, there's a very interesting holiday in Zambia, for example, where you can stay in an animal conservation park.
I Mm. That's a park where they look after wild animals?
S Yes. There are some scientists who work there all the time studying the animals.
I What kind of animals can you find there?
S Oh, er, elephants, lions, er, blue monkey, zebras. And people can stay in the park in tents and watch the scientists at work. We organise walks, river trips, fishing trips, bird watching trips, it's a fantastic holiday.
I Are all your holidays outside Europe?
S Oh no. There's a very good holiday in France, for example. We go hot-air ballooning there. But you have to get up very early in the morning for that, when it's not too windy.
I That sounds wonderful. How long do you stay up in the balloon?
S Oh, about an hour. And everyone can do one or two flights a day.
I I'd love to go on both those holidays. But aren't your holidays all rather expensive?
S No. We have a very good holiday in Sweden, for example. It's a rafting holiday. When you get to Sweden, someone shows you how to make your own raft from tree logs. You bring your own tent, we give you a map of rivers in the area and you travel along the rivers in the raft - where you want - and camp on the riverside. That's a very cheap holiday.

Exercise 6: Not good enough

R Hello, reception, can I help you?
W Yes. This is Mrs Jameson, room 306. I'd like to speak to the manager, please.
R Just one moment, madam, I'll put you through.
M Hello, this is Mr Saville, the manager.
W Ah, this is Mrs Jameson, room 306. I'm calling about my room. I'd like to make a complaint.
M Oh dear, is something wrong?
W Yes, I'm afraid there is. I am not satisfied with my room. It's in a mess. The bed isn't made, there are dirty ashtrays on the table ...
M I am terribly sorry, madam, I'll send someone up right away.
W And there's another thing. The bathroom is dirty and there's a big spider in the washbasin.
M I really must apologise for all this, madam. Let me offer you another room with a 20% discount.
W Well, that'll be fine. Thank you.

Unit 18

Exercise 2: In the family

Part 1

Romance isn't only for young people, you know. Me and George are very romantic, really. We've been married for about six months now. After we got married we wanted, you know, a special holiday. I suppose it's a honeymoon, really. Anyway, we're going to Australia to visit my sister and George's son and grandchildren. His son has been in Australia since 1980, so he hasn't seen him since then. And my sister - well, I haven't seen her since 1962. I mean, we've written, but we haven't met since she went out there. So, anyway, we've planned this big holiday.

Part 2

You see, my daughter's husband died just after the little girl was born and it was very difficult for her, so I've lived here with them since then. I look after my granddaughter during the day while her mum goes to college. She's studying nursing. She was a nurse before, but she hasn't worked for a long time now and, well - so many things have changed since she stopped work. And Robert, that's my grandson, he's been a big help to his mum since his dad died, but he's still at school ...

Part 3

Oh, no. I don't want to live with anyone. My daughter's always asking me to go and live with them, but - no. I want to stay here. I've lived here for fifty odd years, I don't want to move now. I like cooking, reading ... no, I'm fine on my own. I'm never sick. In fact, I haven't been near a doctor for twenty years. Oh, I suppose I might get married. There are a couple of women after me, you know. But, no, I think I'm better off on my own. I can do what I want, you know, please myself.

Exercise 5: A helping hand

Dialogue A

W1 Would you like a seat?
W2 Oh, thank you, that's very kind of you.
W1 Here, let me take your shopping.
W2 Thanks a lot. It's quite heavy.

Dialogue B

M Shall I help you across the street?
W No thanks, I'm quite all right.
M It's no trouble. It's very busy right now.
W I'm fine, really, I can manage by myself.

Dialogue C

M1 Can you manage?
M2 I don't think I can reach those biscuits. They're too high up.
M1 Here. Let me get them for you.
M2 Thanks very much. That's a big help.

Unit 19

Exercise 4: Five Field Kono

W Do you know Five Field Kono?
M No, I don't think so. What kind of game is it?
W It's a Korean board game. You play on a square board divided into 16 squares, four across, four down.
M Yes ...
W You don't have to have a special board. You can use a piece of paper, like this ...
M Mhmm.
W Now each player has seven pieces. You can use buttons or coins, but it's better if they're different colours. One colour for each player.
M OK. Where do you have to put the pieces?
W Well, I put five across the bottom, one on each corner of the squares, like this. And the other two at the sides, one on each side. Then you have to do the same with the other seven pieces at the top. Five across the top and one at each side.
M Like this?
W That's right.
M And how do you play?
W Well, you have to get your pieces to the other side. I have to get my pieces to your side and you have to get your pieces to my side.
M What? You have to move along the lines?
W No, you have to move diagonally across the squares - backwards or forwards.
M Forwards or backwards? Why backwards?
W Because you have to move a piece every time. If you can't go forwards, you have to go backwards. And you can't move if there's another piece already there.
M OK, let's have a game then.
W Right, you start.
M Is it better to go first?
W I'm not telling you. You'll find out when you play.

Exercise 6: Persuading

M1 Who's for a game of cards?
W1 No thanks, I'm no good at cards.
M1 Oh, come on. We'll play something easy.
M2 I'm not playing with you, you always cheat.
M1 Cheat? No, I don't! I'm just lucky.
W2 Huh, you usually win, and it's not always good luck. No, I don't feel like it anyway ...
M1 OK. OK. No cheating. Come on, let's have just one game.
W1 Oh, all right then, just one game.
M1 How about you two? Go on. A quick game. You can choose what we play.
W1 Go on then, we'll play. But just one game.
M1 Right, I'll shuffle. You say which game you want.

Unit 20

Exercise 4: Sea zoo

I When did this Sea Zoo open?
M About three years ago. Sea zoos are very popular now, especially with children. You see, children who don't live near the sea never normally see these creatures. But now they can come here, see lots of sea creatures and plants, read about them and even touch some of them.
I Which ones are the most popular?
M Oh, the sharks, I think. Children know about sharks and they're usually afraid of them. So they like to see them close up, you know, to see their teeth - behind the glass screen, of course. And the lobsters. I think because they can pick them up and look closely at them. Lobsters are very strange looking things, with their long pincers at the front. And children sometimes know that lobsters will eat each other if they're hungry, so some children watch the lobsters for hours, waiting to see if this will happen.
I Oh dear. I don't think I'd like that.
M And another popular one is the octopus. You know an octopus will change colour if it's in danger. It can change to match it's surroundings so that the attackers can't see it.
I I didn't know that.
M Oh yes, it's wonderful to watch. And, of course, it's such a strange looking creature with its large eyes, long arms and rubbery body.
I I know that octopuses will release a black liquid in the water if something attacks them.
M That's right. If something attacks an octopus it will shoot off at a great speed and let out the black liquid. The black liquid makes a kind of cloud behind the octopus so the attacker can't see very well and the liquid also contains a chemical with a strong smell. The attacker will follow the smell of the chemical and not of the octopus itself.
I It's a very good defence, isn't it.
M Yes, it is. And another thing people often don't know about octopuses is that when the female lays her eggs she will guard them for weeks and as soon as the eggs hatch, the female will die.
I Really? ...

Exercise 6: Strange pets

Dialogue A

W There was a woman on the radio talking about her pet spiders.
M What? She keeps spiders as pets?
W Yes, it was really interesting.
M Ugh! No, not spiders.
W Why, what's wrong?
M I can't stand spiders, I'm terrified of them.

Dialogue B

M We're looking after my cousin's snake.
W What? In your house?
M Yes, but it's in a cage.
W Oh no.
M Come and see.
W No, really. I'm scared of snakes.
M It's asleep.
W No. I couldn't look at it.

Nelson English Language Teaching
100 Avenue Road
London NW3 3HF

An International Thomson Publishing Company

London • Bonn • Boston • Madrid • Melbourne • Mexico City •
New York • Paris • Singapore • Tokyo

First published by Collins ELT
ISBN 0-00-370500-5

This edition first published by Nelson ELT,
a division of Thomas Nelson and Sons Ltd 1993

ISBN 0-17-55565279
NPN 9 8 7 6 5 4 3

Printed in Hong Kong

Acknowledgements

The publishers are grateful to the following for permission to reproduce the copyright material on the pages indicated.

Four facts from *The Guinness Book of Records* (p 30), Copyright © **Guinness Publishing Ltd 1989**; letter adapted from extract from *Traveller's Tales* by Eric Newby (p 26), **HarperCollins Publishers Ltd**; text adapted from article 'Picture Perfect' by Bob Pool (p 13), **Los Angeles Times Syndicate**; texts adapted from articles 'Quickstep Across Africa' by Pearson Philllips (p 5) and 'Put Two and Two Together' by Rodney Tyler (p 29), **Mail on Sunday/You Magazine**; text based on 'A Room of My Own' featuring Roger Doudna (p 4), **Observer**; text on Operation Raleigh (p 6), **Operation Raleigh**; text based on article 'Architecture, Japanese City of the Future' (p 31), Joanna Pitman; information on Weddings in Paradise (p 23), **Worldwide Thomson**.

Photographs

J Allan Cash Ltd (p 33); All-Sport (U.K.) Ltd (p 2); Aspect Picture Library Ltd (p 21); BBC Photographic Library (p 7); Bridgeman Art Library Ltd (p 15); Camera Press Ltd (p 36); C.O.I. (p 11); Cephas Picture Library (p 35); The Cinema Museum (p 7); Bruce Coleman Ltd (p 17); Colorific! Telegraph Colour Library (pp 24,29); Colorsport (p 27); Terry Cryer (p 11); Flora Duff-Torrance (p 33); E.T. Archive (p 27); Eric Ellington (p 4); Greg Evans International (Photo Library) (p 25); Mary Evans Picture Library (p 15); Sally and Richard Greenhill (pp 1, 2, 11, 35); Susan Griggs Agency Ltd (pp 1, 2, 21, 23, 28); Robert Harding Picture Library Ltd (pp 3, 11, 16); The Hulton Picture Company (p 15); The Hutchison Library (p 23); The Image Bank (pp 3, 21, 33, 34); Images Colour Library Ltd (p 23); International Stock Exchange Photo Library (pp 1, 21); The Kobal Collection Ltd (p 27); The Mansell Collection (p 15); NHPA (p 17); Network Photographers (p 1); Orpix (p 2); Popperfoto (p 16); Rex Features Ltd (pp 23, 28); Tony Stone Worldwide Photo Library (pp 3, 17, 23, 35); Universal Pictorial Press and Agency Ltd (p 28); The Vintage Magazine Co Ltd (p 16); World Pictures (p 25)
All other photos by Sue Baker.

Picture research by Mandy Twells.

Illustrations

Paul Bateman (pp 13, 31); Ken Binder - Satchel Illustrators (pp 9/10, 37); Christina Brimage (pp 15/16, 21, 27/28, 29, 35); David Brindley (pp 7/8); Richard Draper (pp 14, 32, 57); Angelica Elsebach (pp 39/40); Antonia Enthoven (pp 4, 18, 22, 30, 36); Sue Hillwood-Harris (pp 5/6); Tania Hurt-Newton (pp 12, 22, 27, 32, 34, 40, 41, 43, 47, 51); Jo Lawrence (pp 19/20); Joanna Quinn (pp 48, 49, 55, 60); Tracey Ramsdale (p 18); Sue Shields (p 4); Emma Sutherland (pp 25/26); all airbrush work by John Gilkes.

The publishers have made every effort to contact owners of copyright. They apologise for any omissions, and if details are sent, will be glad to rectify these when the title is reprinted.

Design

Shireen Nathoo